25 Gunfighter Patterns
FOR CARVERS

Al Streetman

with photography by Jack Lisiecki

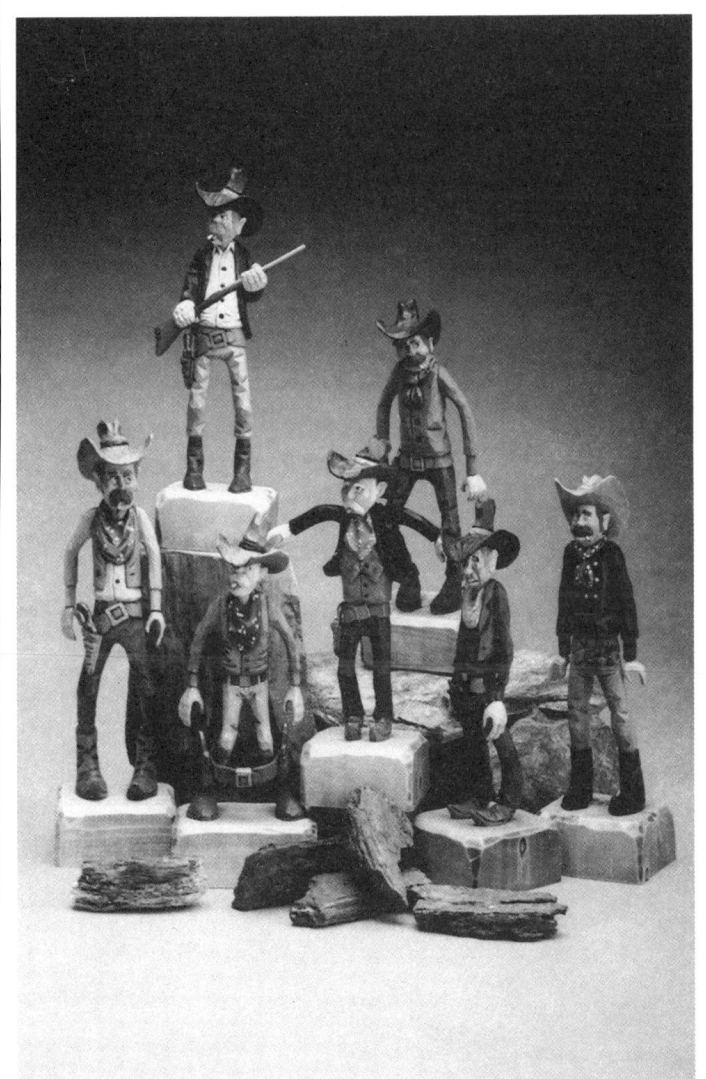

With step-by-step
carving instructions

AF271652

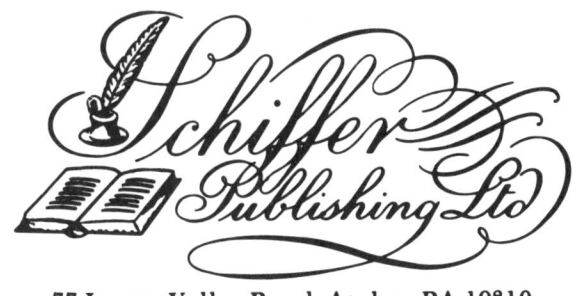

Schiffer Publishing Ltd

77 Lower Valley Road, Atglen, PA 19310

ACKNOWLEDGEMENTS

The following people helped make this book possible. I thank you all.

Jack Lisiecki: Once more, your photography was superb.

Marilynn Jones: For your continued word-processing support, both in data entry, and especially in data retrieval.

Delta Technical Coatings, Inc.: The paint samples for the gunfighters were excellent, and satisfactory in all respects.

Wood Carvers Supply, Inc., Englewood, Florida: High quality carving tools and supplies.

Library of Congress Cataloging-in-Publication Data

Streetman, Al.
     25 gunfighter patterns for carvers/Al
Streetman; with photography by Jack Lisiecki.
          p. cm. -- (A Schiffer book for woodcarvers)
     ISBN 0-88740-783-8 (pbk.)
     1. Wood-carving --Patterns. 2. Wood-carved
figurines. 3. Cowboys in art. I. Title. II. Series.
TT199.7.S787   1995
731.4'62--dc20   95-10801
                                                      CIP

Published by Schiffer Publishing, Ltd.
77 Lower Valley Road
Atglen, PA 19310
Please write for a free catalog.
This book may be purchased from the publisher.
Please include $2.95 postage.
Try your bookstore first.

We are interested in hearing from authors
with book ideas on related subjects.

BOOK DESIGN BY AUDREY L. WHITESIDE.

Printed in China
ISBN: 0-88740-783-8

DEDICATION

To Meg and Rachel, both of you are a joy and a blessing.

CONTENTS

INTRODUCTION

Anywhere you find a group of woodcarvers, you're bound to find at least one who is busy carving a cowboy, and in many instances, carving a gunfighter of some type. The western character has always held some appeal for us, and there seems to be a mystique associated with the gunfighters. They are portrayed as rugged individuals in the movies, and sometimes, they are even portrayed as the "good guy".

The gunfighters in this book are not the most handsome the world has ever seen, and I suspect that a few of them might even be past their "prime", but you wouldn't want to tangle with any of them. I searched high and low for one who would agree to pose as my model for the carving project (he is so ornery that he wouldn't allow me to use his name), and the others will be hopping mad when they find out I drew them in the pattern section.

I believe you will have fun carving them. Once you get a few carved and painted, they will make a colorful addition to your collection of characters. They tend to get a bit rowdy from time to time, but you'll just have to learn to live with it.

In the carving chapter, I will be sharing some of my tricks and secrets regarding head and hat carving, hand carving, and gun carving. I hope the methods I use and teach will give you some new insight into character carving techniques, and will make carving easier and more fun for you.

Some of you "old-timers" and veteran woodcarvers may observe that my carving project is not as complex or detailed as you might carve it. **There is a method to my madness.** In this book, as in the Santa and Uncle Sam books, I have tried to design a project that would yield a nice result, yet not be so complex or involved that the *beginning wood carver* will be unable to accomplish it. I want to reach as many wood carvers as possible, and share the joy of carving with them. As the beginners gain more experience, they can add additional details as desired.

Except for the actual carving project, I have not included specific carving instructions. I have found that each carver has his or her own style, and each has their preference for which tool to use in a particular area, or to achieve a particular effect.

Rather than giving a vague instruction such as "use a small gouge," I have listed the particular size gouge I used in the different steps of the carving project, as we move through each step of the carving. This is more for the benefit of the beginning carver, than the more experienced ones. If you don't have these particular sizes of gouges or tools, use something similar. The world won't come to a crashing end if you don't use the same exact tools I used.

The patterns in this book include approximate dimensions of the side and front views, if you desire to carve them to the same size as I originally designed them. You will notice that the thickest wood I use in the side profile is 2 inches, except for one pattern which required slightly larger wood due to the position the gunfighter is in. Most wood carving sources carry 1-3/4" and 2" thick wood, so it is fairly easy to obtain. If you desire a larger or smaller version, simply enlarge or shrink the pattern on a photocopying machine. You may also want to use the photocopying machine to make several sizes of the hand template. This way you will be sure to have a hand outline that is the proper size for the gunfighter you carve.

You will notice that the patterns contain several drawings: a side and front profile with dimensions, which is the pattern you will use to saw out the body blank; a head pattern; and a pistol or rifle pattern, depending on the pattern you are going to carve. The numbers on the arms of the patterns correspond to numbers on the hand template, and are the suggested hands to use for that pattern. If you would rather use different hands, feel free to do so. This will allow you to achieve many different looks from just a few patterns. Each pattern also shows some assembled views of the pieces, so you can picture how the head, body, and guns might look if you desire to carve that pattern.

Before you begin the actual carving project, I **highly recommend** that you read through the entire book at least once. You may notice that a detail that was not completely clear to you in the carving section may become **very clear** in the painting section. Often the details show up much better once the wood has been given some life with a coat of paint. *Remember*, if we carve it in the first part of the book, we'll paint it later, so you have at least two sections of the book for a reference. Many of these characters will also show up in the gallery and study model section, so that will give you a third source for a reference.

I use Basswood whenever possible, but any soft wood such as Jelutong, clear Spruce, or Sugar/White Pine will work equally well. If possible, use a bandsaw with a 1/8" blade to cut out the side and front profiles. (On the patterns with extended arms, you may choose to saw out the arms separately, so as to make maximum use of the wood grain direction, then attach them to the body before doing your final carving). The bandsaw will allow you to release the rough version of the gunfighter from the block of wood faster than trying to use a coping saw or other means to cut out the pattern.

GENERAL NOTES

1. Trace the head, body and gun patterns, or make a copy of them on a photocopying machine. Glue the patterns you copied or traced onto some heavy paper such as poster paper or a manila file folder. When the glue is dry, cut out the patterns. This method will prevent you from ruining the master patterns in your book. Also, make a copy of the hand template, glue it to some heavy paper, and cut it out. We will use it at a later step in the carving project, when it is time to make the hands and fit them to the body.

2. Lay your pattern on the wood, trace the outline of it, and saw it out. Remember my note about the patterns with extended arms.

3. You should now have a rough blank ready to be carved.

4. Use your own techniques and style to bring the carving to the finished stage.

5. You will notice that the patterns to be used for sawing out the body do not show the hands attached. This method allows you to carve the body, then decide on the size and style of hands you want to use for that carving. (This is where you will put the hand template to work). Many times the type of hands will be determined by which accessories you will include with the carving (rifle, coffee cup, etc). Because you are carving the hands separately from the body, you can orient them to take advantage of the wood grain when you saw them out. This will allow you endless variations of hand positions, so you can give more life to your carvings. Also, if you are creating an extreme caricature, you can use a larger than normal hand pattern to add more humor to the carving.

6. We are also going to carve the head separately from the main body. This gives you several advantages: (1) if you make a mistake on the head or body, the other part won't be ruined ; (2) you can assemble the head to the body looking straight ahead, or you can turn it to one side (turning the head to one side will give more "life" to your carvings); (3) You can "mix and match" different heads with different bodies, therefore gaining more variations from a given number of patterns.

7. The pistols and/or rifles will be carved last. Carving them as separate pieces lets you orient them to get maximum strength from the grain direction, and gives you more flexibility in positioning them on the body.

PROJECT CARVING TOOLS

For those of you who may want to duplicate the cuts I made using the same tools, I have listed the tools used in the carving project.

1/8" #39 V gouge	3mm #3 Flat gouge
1/4" #39 V gouge	10mm #3 Flat gouge
3mm #41 V gouge	6mm #4 Curved gouge
2mm #10 U gouge	6mm #10 U gouge
3mm #10 U gouge	3mm #7 U gouge

TIPS

1. EYES

A. I often use various sizes of plastic-head quilting pins to make eyes. Mark where you want the eyes to be on the finished carving. Using a drill and bit that is slightly larger than the pin head you are going to use, make a hole for each eye.

Using wire cutters, snip off the pin head, leaving about 1/4" of the pin attached to the head.

Insert the pin head into the eye socket, with the pin end going in first. Use a nail set to seat the head into the hole until only a small orb protrudes. This gives a fairly realistic eye without too much effort on your part. For extra detail, remove a triangular-shaped piece of wood at each side of the pin head. This will make a very realistic eye when it is painted.

B. A second easy way to create eyes is to use carver's eye punches. Select the size eye punch you want to use, based on the size of the eye sockets you have made. Push the eye punch against the socket firmly and rotate it. After making both eyes, remove triangular-shaped pieces of wood from the corners to give more detail.

C. The most realistic way to make eyes begins with carving the eye sockets so that about a 90° angle is formed. Lightly sketch in a football-shaped eye in each socket, so that the top half of the football is on the upper half of the socket, and the lower half of the football is on the lower half of the socket. When you sketch in the footballs, make the outside ends lower than the inside ends. Having the eyes slanted a small amount will help give your gunfighter that mean, gnarly look.

Using the tip of your knife, score the football outline to a depth of about 1/16". Now use the tip of your knife to remove triangular-shaped pieces of wood from the left and right corner of each eye. This will leave a small section of wood inside each football, which will be the eyeball. You can vary the way you remove the triangular-shaped corners, if you want the eyes to be looking more to one side, rather than straight ahead.

One last thing concerning eyes: Don't get upset if you discover that you have carved one eye smaller or at a different angle than the other eye. Depending on how war-weary or worn and torn you want to depict your character, this "accident" may work to your advantage. It will lend an interesting variation to the carving, and no one has to know you didn't do it that way on purpose!!

2. When buying wood, whether it be Basswood, Spruce, or some other type, try to pick the **lightest** pieces. They tend to have less fat and sap in them, so they are **easier** to carve.

3. I normally use the same thickness of wood for the head as I use for the body. This provides plenty of wood for a big floppy hat brim.

4. When making a rifle for your carving, it is easier and more realistic if you make the barrel separate from the stock. The best material for the barrel is 1/16" aluminum tubing which can be purchased at any hobby or hardware store. To cut it to length, simply roll it lightly back and forth under your knife blade. It is a soft metal and won't hurt your knife edge. After carving the wood stock, a small amount of cement such as Ambroid™ or DuPont™ will hold the barrel firmly in place. An alternate method for the barrel is to use a section of 1/8" wood dowel, glued in place and painted silver.

5. If you want your gunfighter to have a "scruffy" look, rather than a well-manicured look, you may want to add some beard stubble to the cheek, chin and neck areas. This may be done by pricking small pieces of wood loose using a very tiny "V" gouge (such as a **2mm #39** gouge), or by making small indentations in the wood using the sharpened tip of a small finishing nail or electric engraving tool. An alternate method, if you prefer, is to add the stubble detail using a burning device such as a Hot Tool™, Detail Master™, etc.

After painting the flesh and hair color, *very lightly* dry-brush a small amount of black onto the beard stubble area, to give that 5 o'clock shadow look. If you have painted the hair gray or white to depict an old grizzly gunfighter, you may want to dry-brush small amounts of black *and* gray onto the beard stubble area.

6. If you want your gunfighter to have a dusty, trail-worn appearance, *lightly* dry-brush *small* amounts of gray or white paint all over the carving. This will help remove the "new" look from his clothing and accessories.

7. An easy way to help determine where you want to place some wrinkles and folds in the arms, torso and legs is to observe and note where the wood grain changes direction as you are carving. Usually in the crook of an elbow or behind the knees, you will notice that wood "fuzzies" try to appear, no matter how carefully you carve or how sharp your knife is. This is because the wood grain direction is changing, and in one direction or the other, you are trying to carve against the grain, lifting the end grain. These spots are perfect candidates for wrinkles and folds, made with a large "V" tool or by cutting wedges out with your knife. As a beginning carver, if you do nothing more than add a few cuts in these areas, you will be amazed at the difference in the way the carving looks. With experience, you will start noticing other places to add wrinkles and folds, and some day you will be the best carver in the world!

8. For those of you who have never had much practice enlarging or reducing patterns, or being able to calculate how much enlargement or reduction you need to select on the photocopying machine, here are some general guidelines:

Let's say you have a pattern that shows a side profile requiring 2" thick wood, and you want to make the pattern larger so it will fit on 3" thick wood. Use the following formula to calculate what percentage enlargement to select on the copier:

[New Dimension Desired ÷ Present Dimension] x 100 = %

Using our example, this would work out as follows:

[3" ÷ 2"] x 100 = **150%**.

Going the other way, let's say you have a pattern that shows a 2" side profile, and you want to reduce it down so it will fit on a piece of 1-3/4" thick wood. Using the same formula, it works out as follows:

[1.75" ÷ 2"] x 100 = **87.5%**.

If the machine you are using won't cut large enough or small enough to get the job done on the first try, additional steps may be required. Go ahead and make your first copy using the largest enlargement or reduction setting you can select. Measure the **new** dimensions on your *copy,* **(which will now be your Present Dimension)**, then use the same formula as before to calculate how much additional enlargement or reduction is needed to get the pattern to the size you desired it to be.

GENERAL PAINTING SUGGESTIONS FOR GUNFIGHTERS IN THIS BOOK

I have included some *suggested* colors for all patterns. If you have a preference for a different color scheme, by all means use it. After all, it's your gunfighter, and you can dress him any way you desire (just don't dress him funny, or he'll get mad!).

I have also listed the colors produced by Delta Technical Coatings, Inc., and their identification numbers, which I have found to be suitable for painting these carvings. I have used these colors, and the results were excellent. I hope this will help minimize your confusion when trying to sort through the maze of paint brands and colors at your hobby or craft store.

You may have heard and read this a million times, but when painting your carvings, keep the word **THIN** in mind. What you want to do is stain the wood to give it some color and life, but you don't want the paint so thick that it covers up the beauty of the wood. **NOTE:** When painting the head and hands, I generally use a little thicker mixture of paint than I use on the rest of the carving. I want the face to be a bit more intense than the rest of the carving, since the head and face is what sets most of the mood for the carving.

White #2505
Sandstone #2402
Antique White #2001
Black #2506
Charcoal #2436
Fleshtone #2019
Burnt Sienna #2030
Burnt Umber #2025
Walnut #2024
Blue Heaven #2037
Crocus Yellow #2459
Denim Blue #2477
Crimson #2076
Navy Blue #2089
Quaker Grey #2057
Silver #2603
Red Iron Oxide #2020
Territorial Beige #2425
Cadet Gray #2426
Autumn Brown #2055
GP Purple #2091
Pigskin #2093
Trail Tan #2435
Palomino Tan #2108
Lilac Dusk #2403
Persimmon #2480
Warm Brown Antiquing Gel
Clear Satin Varnish

VEST: Quaker Gray, with a small amount of Charcoal and Silver dry-brushed over the Quaker Gray.

BUTTONS ON VEST, COATS, AND SHIRTS: Black, Silver, or a color of your choice.

PANTS: Denim Blue, Sandstone, or a color of your choice.

BANDANNAS: Crimson, with Crocus Yellow dots; Navy Blue with White dots; Crocus Yellow with Crimson dots, or a color and pattern of your choice.

CIGARETTES: Antique White, with Quaker Gray ash on tip.

BOOTS: Autumn Brown, Black, Burnt Umber, Red Iron Oxide, or a color of your choice.

GUNBELTS, HOLSTER, BELTS: Burnt Sienna, Black, Red Iron Oxide, or a color of your choice.

BELT BUCKLES: Silver.

PISTOLS: Silver, with Walnut hand grips.

RIFLE: Silver barrel and trigger area, with Walnut butt and stock.

FACE, EARS, NECK AND HANDS: Fleshtone.

EYES: White base. Then paint a dot of Blue Heaven in the center, corner or top of eye. Next, paint a smaller dot of Black in the Blue dot. Finally, use a toothpick and put a White highlight on the edge of the Black dot. In the section where I paint the carving project, I'll go into more detail on placing the highlight, depending on where the eye is looking.

HAIR, MUSTACHE AND EYEBROWS: White, Black, Brown or a color of your choice.

HATS: Black, Pigskin, Trail Tan, Cadet Gray, Quaker Gray, Burnt Umber, or a color of your choice. If a hatband was also carved, paint it a contrasting color to the hat so it will show up.

COATS: Denim Blue, Black, Palomino Tan, Territorial Beige, or a color of your choice.

SHIRTS: Crimson, White, Persimmon, Lilac Dusk, GP Purple, or a color of your choice.

PATTERNS

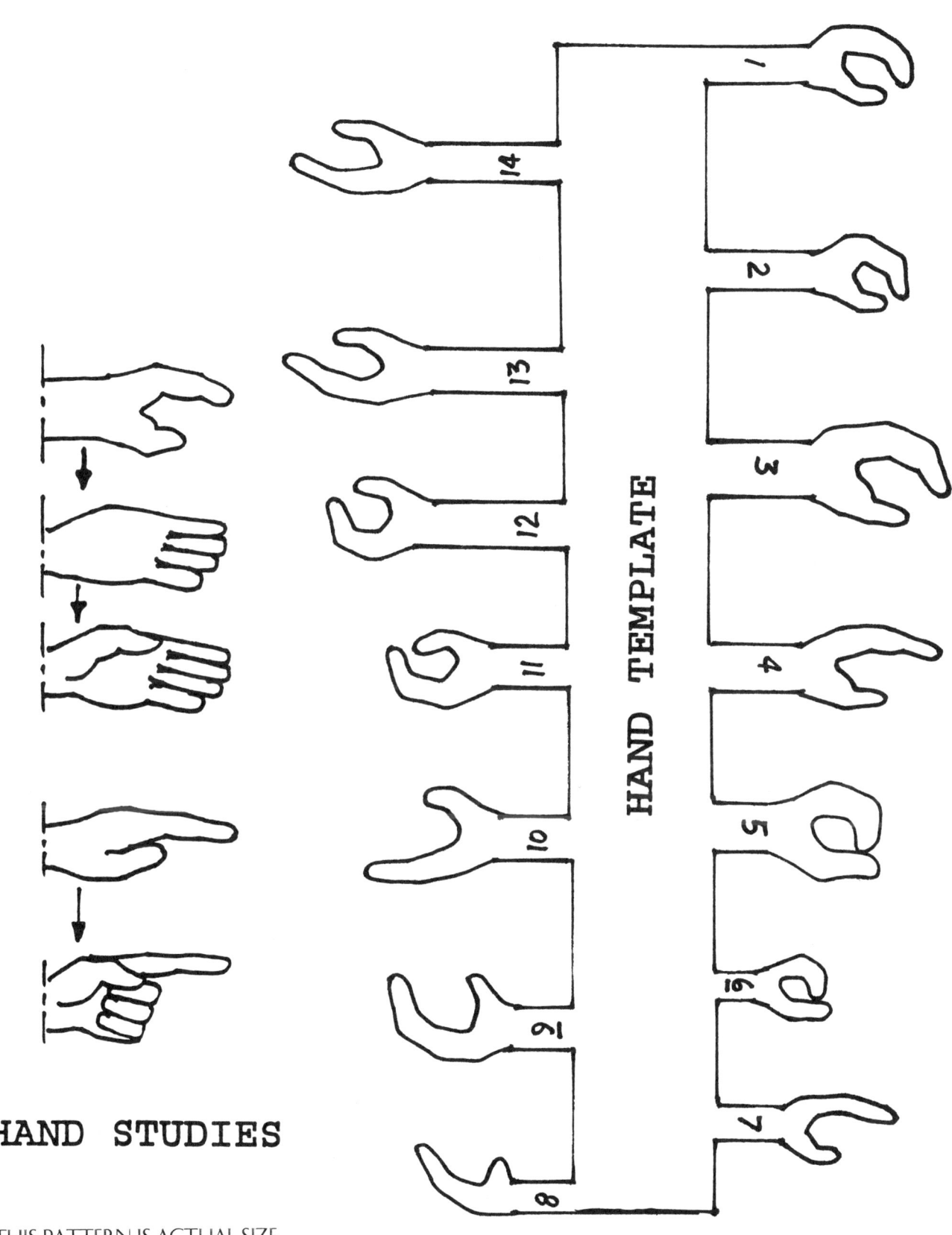

HAND TEMPLATE

HAND STUDIES

THIS PATTERN IS ACTUAL SIZE.

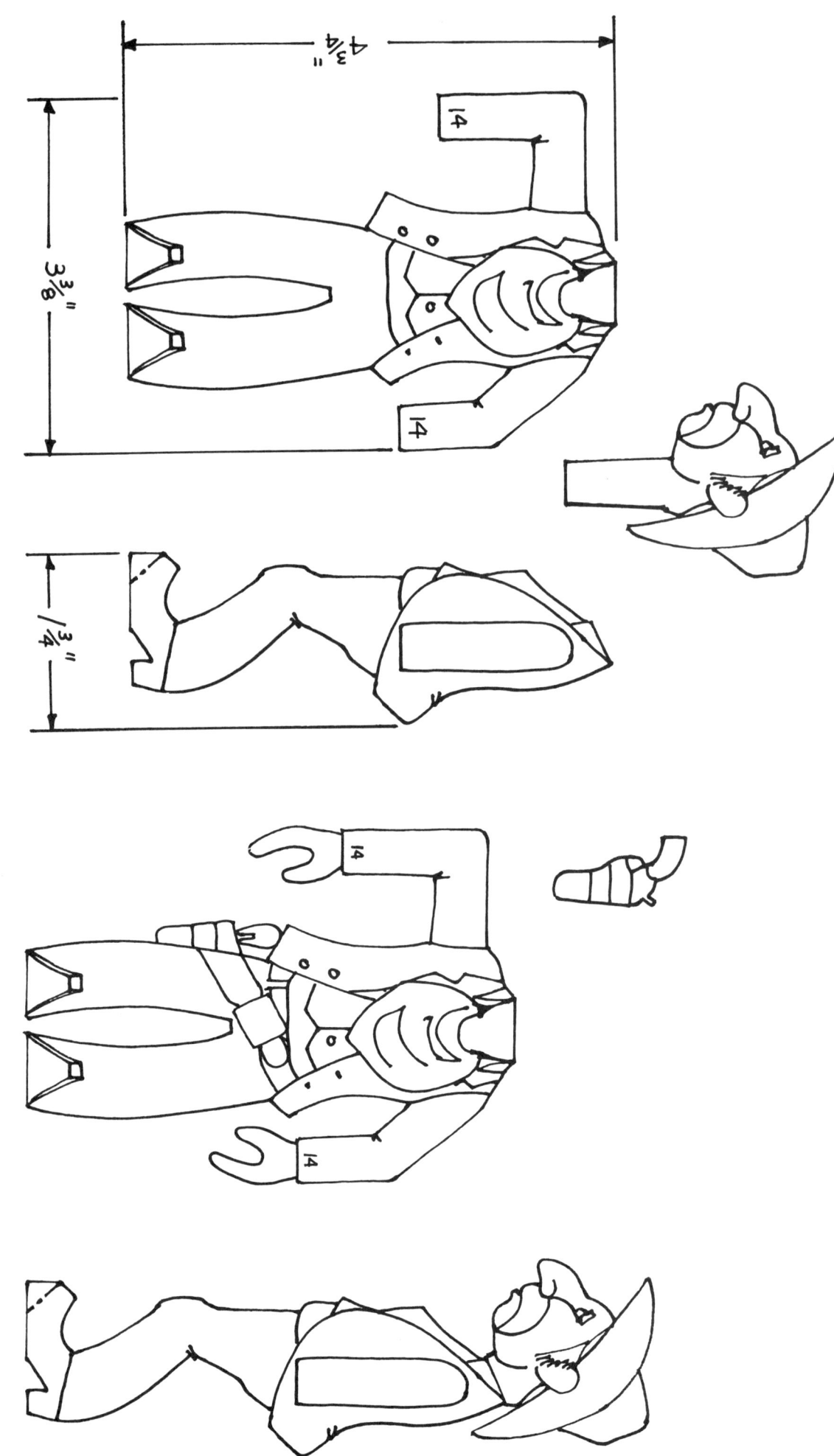

3³⁄₈"

4³⁄₈"

1³⁄₄"

14

14

14

14

ENLARGE THIS PATTERN 133% FOR ORIGINAL SIZE.

THE ARIZONA KID

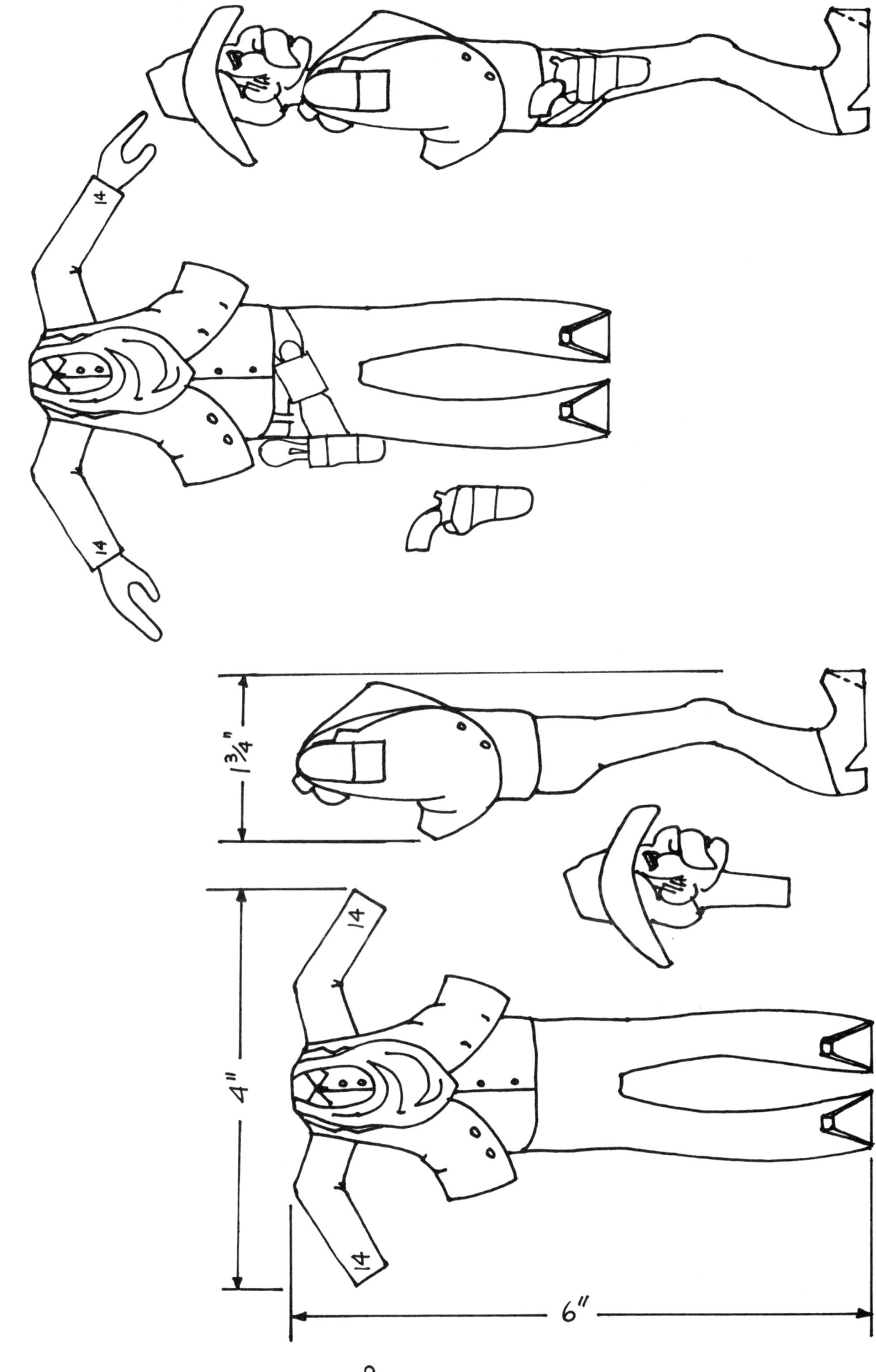

9

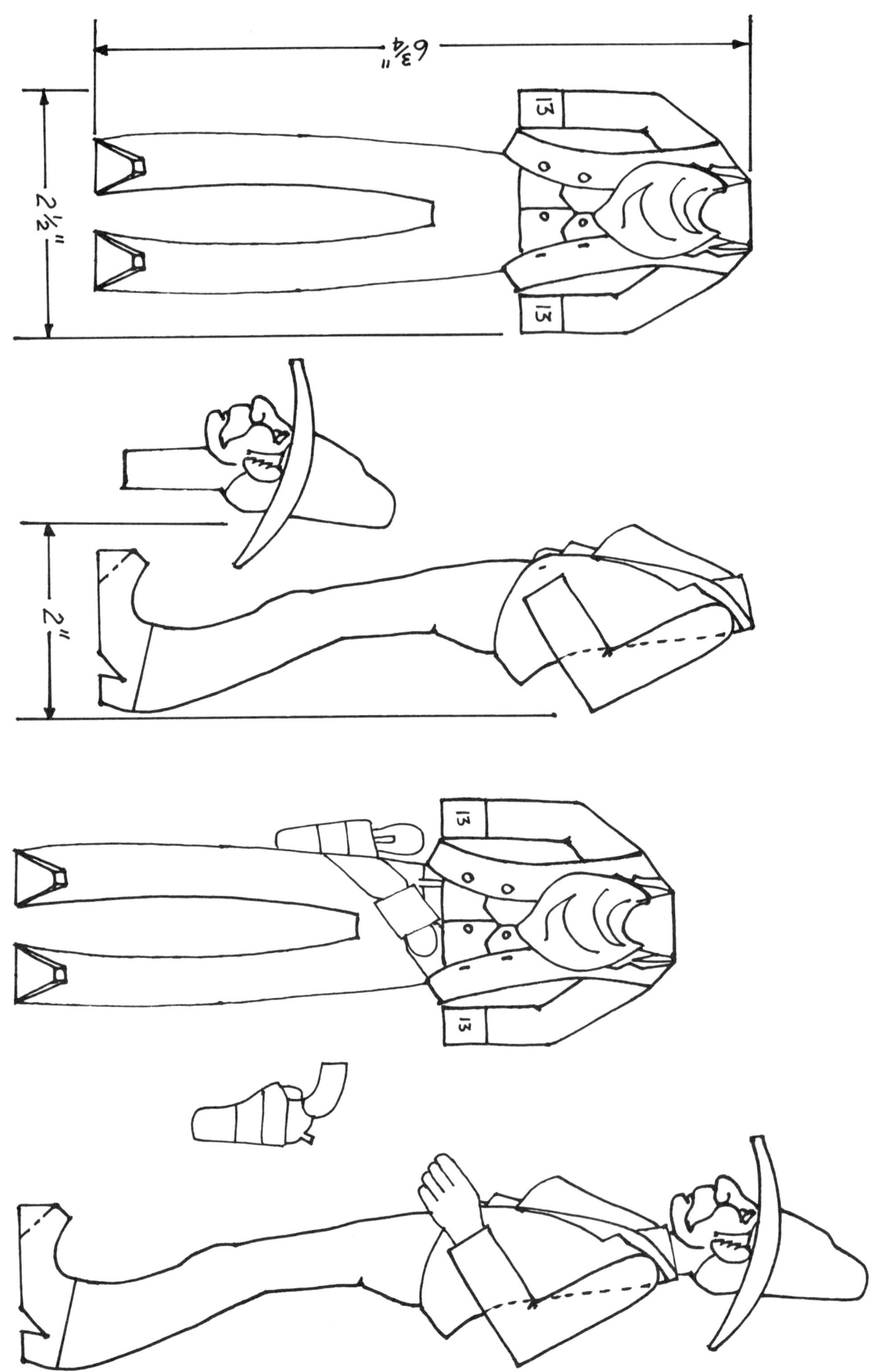

6¾"

2½"

2"

13

13

13

13

ENLARGE THIS PATTERN 133% FOR ORIGINAL SIZE.

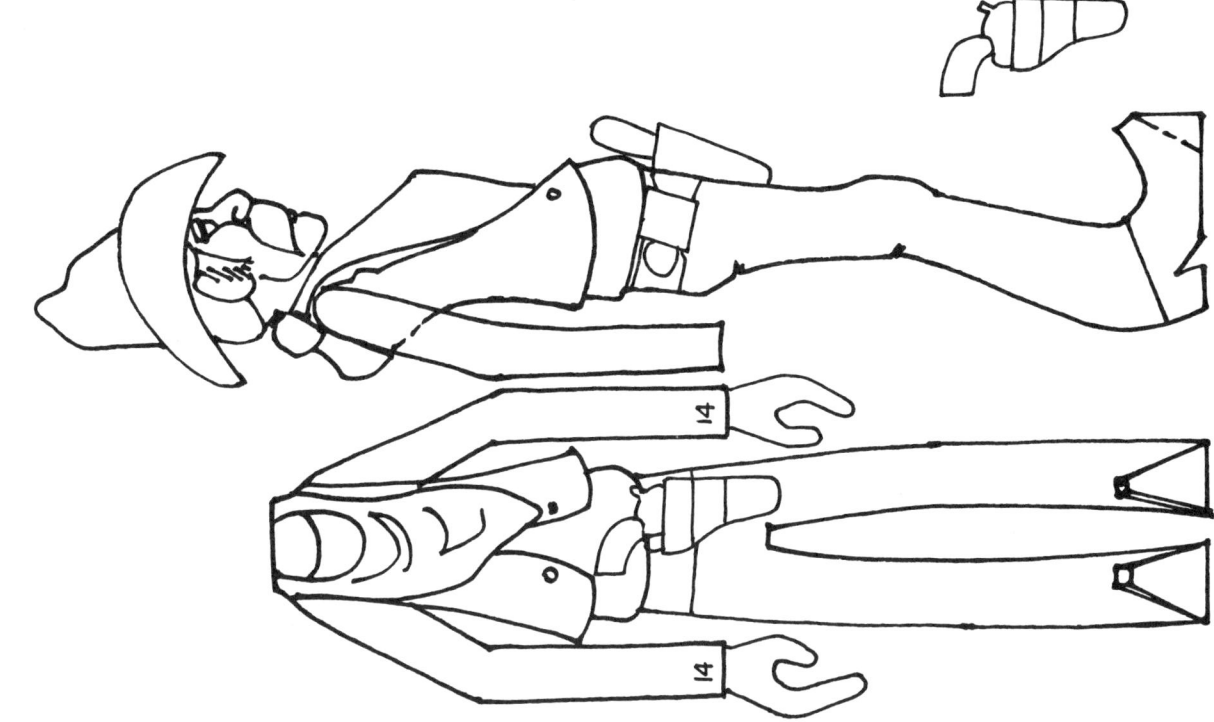

HIPSHOT GEORGE

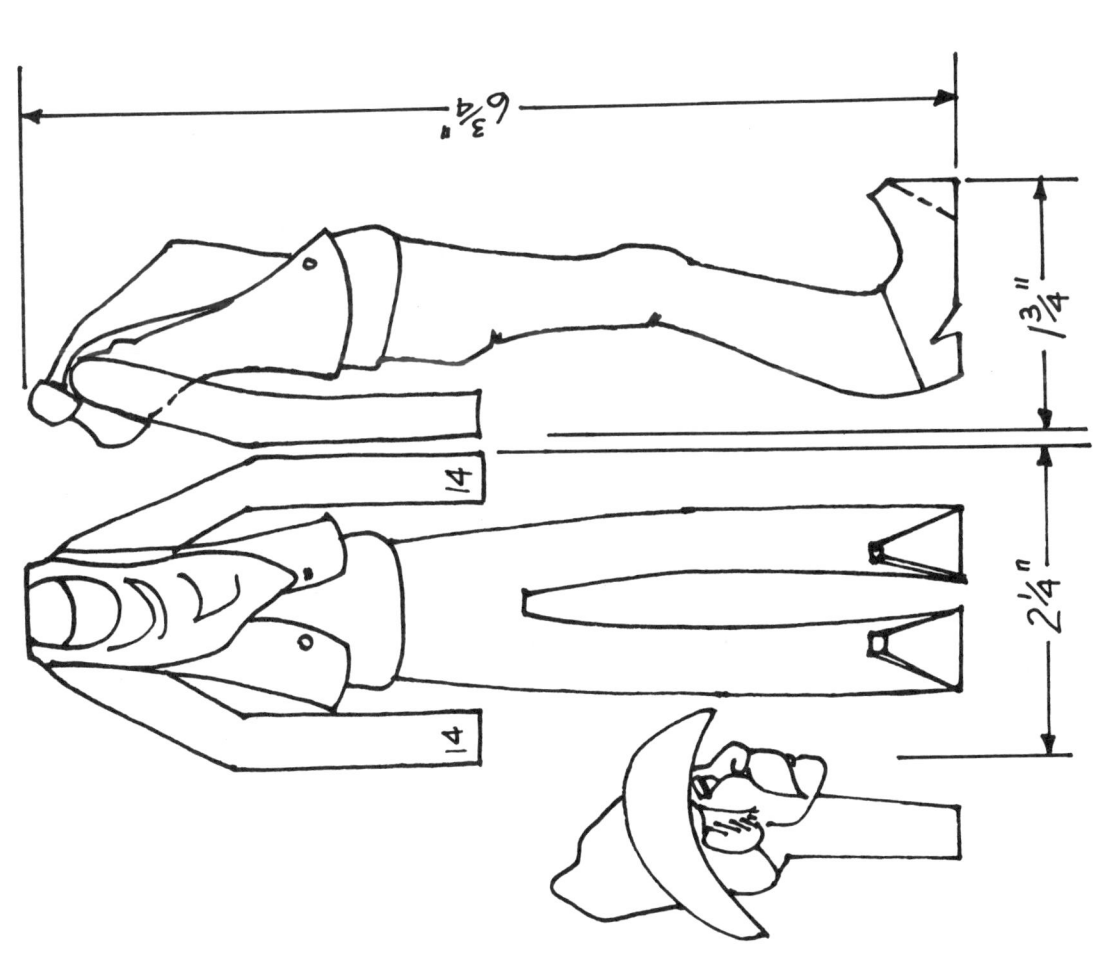

6¼"

5"

14

14

1½"

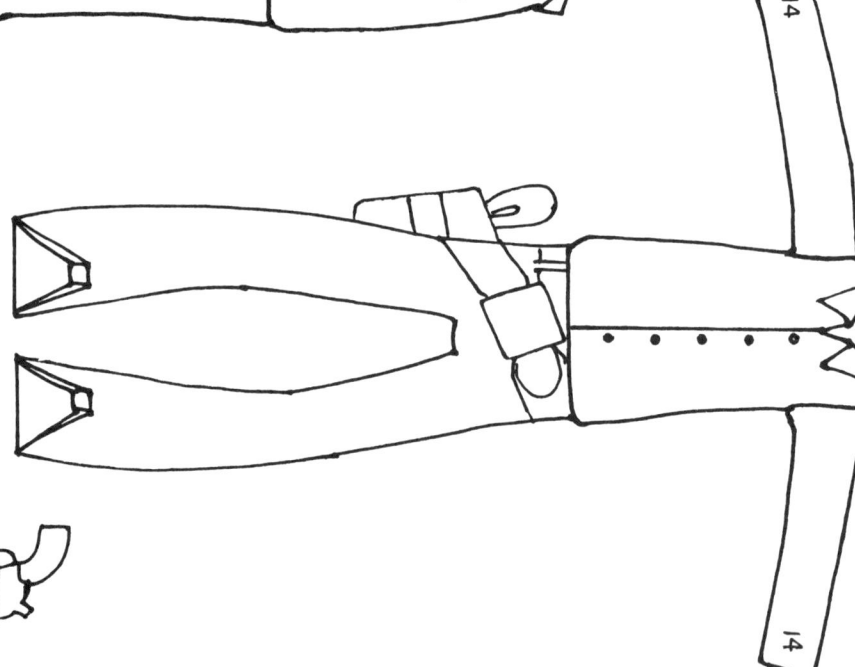

14

14

ENLARGE THIS PATTERN 133% FOR ORIGINAL SIZE.

WILDCAT HEMMONS

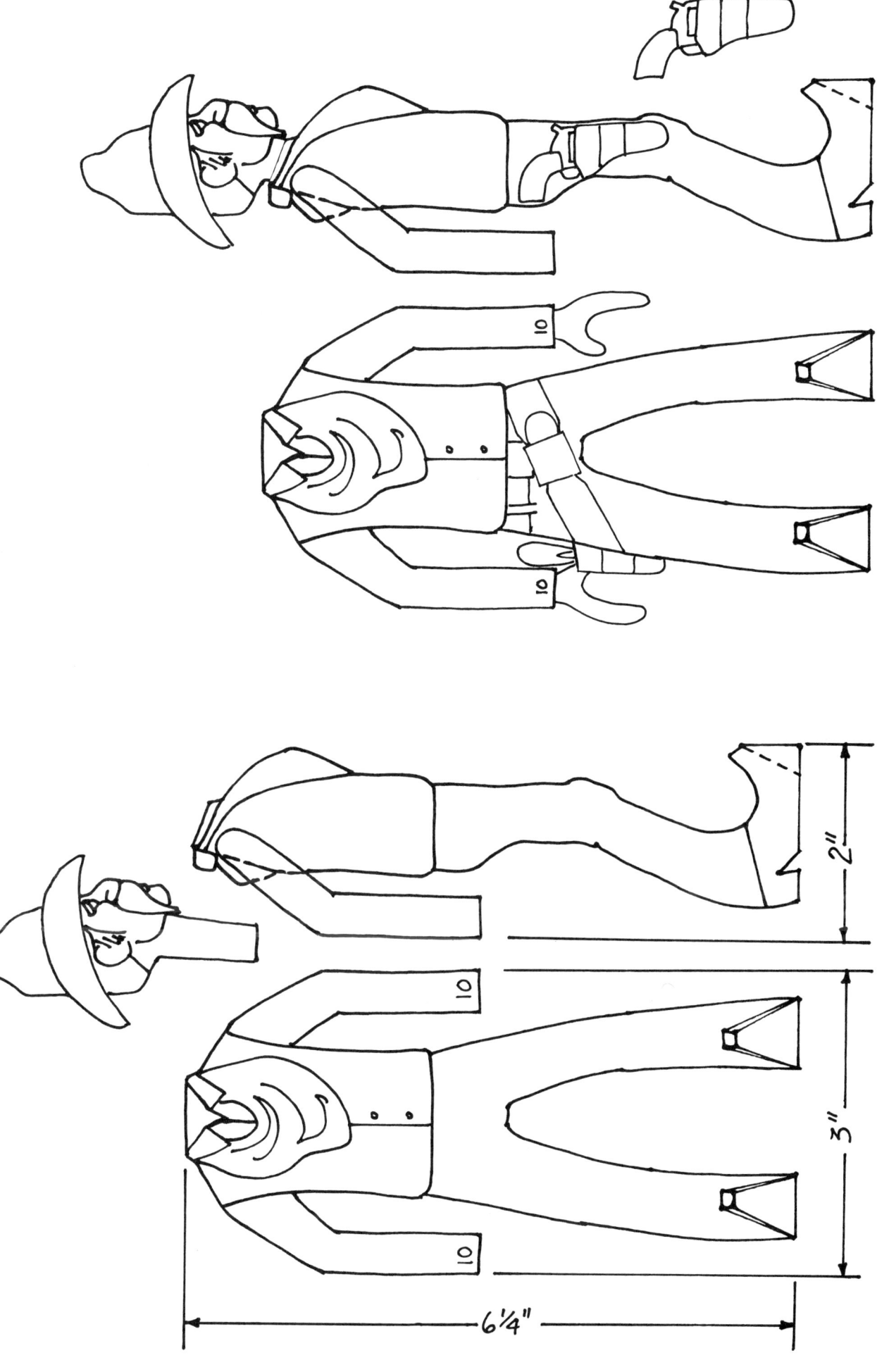

5 5/8"

1 3/4"

2"

14

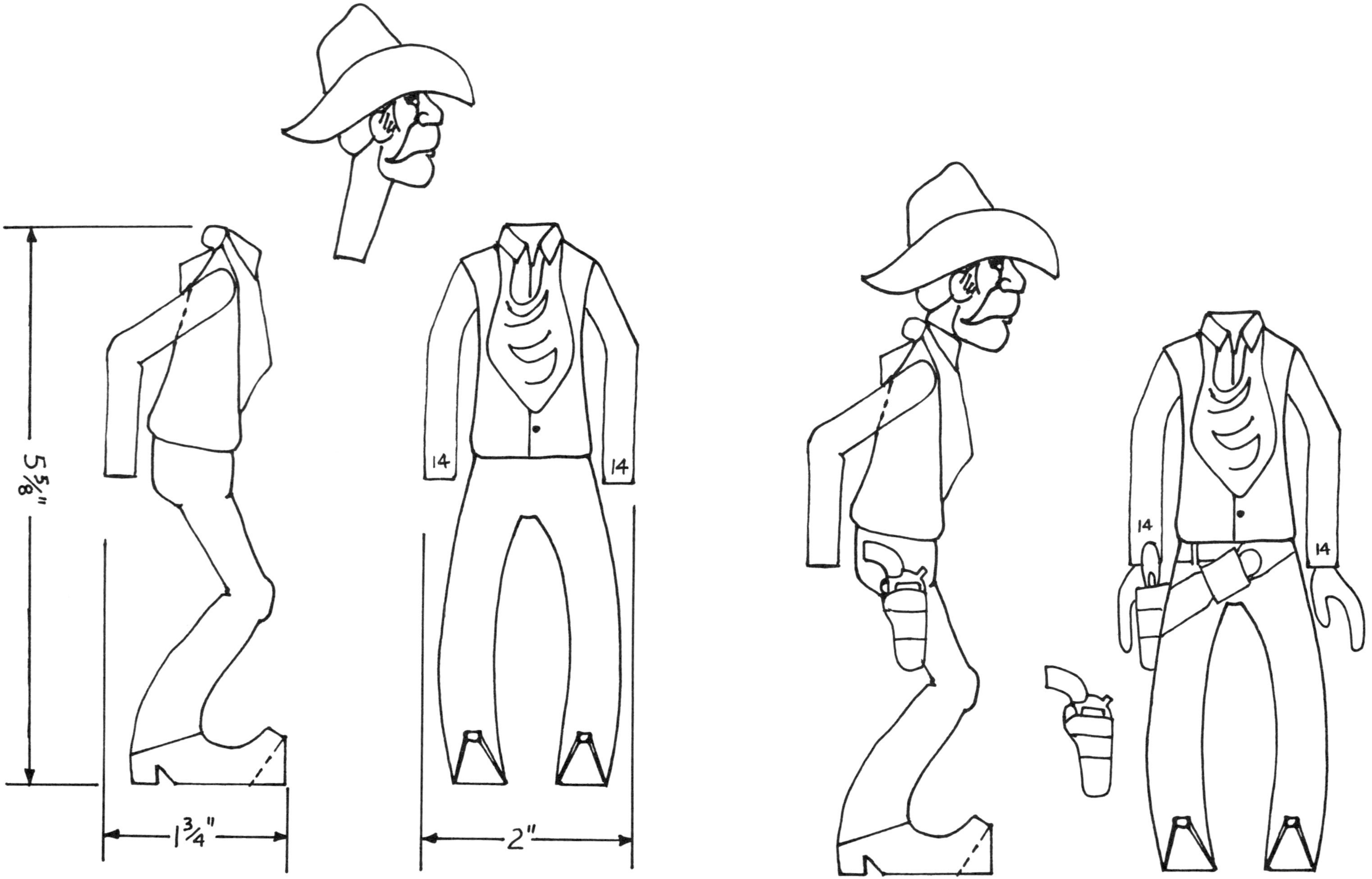

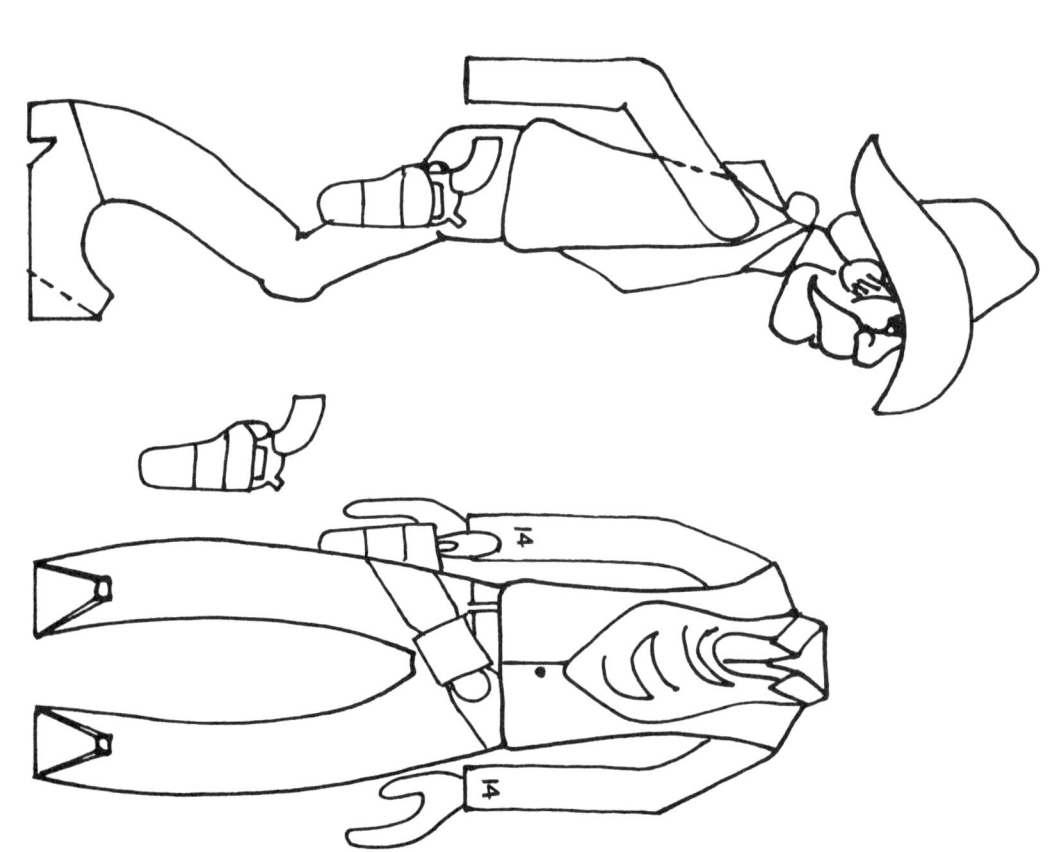

THE REGULATOR

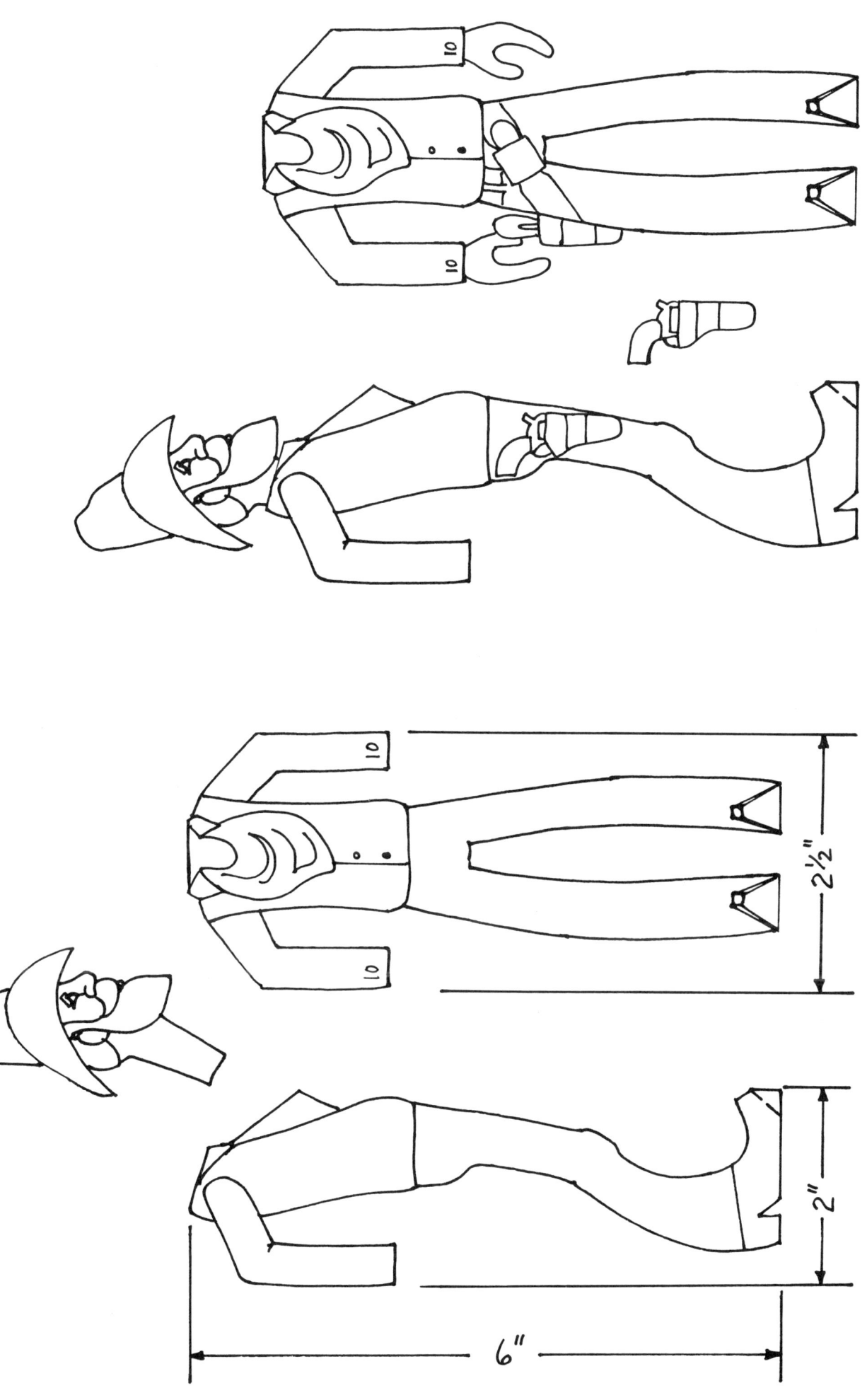

2½"

2"

6"

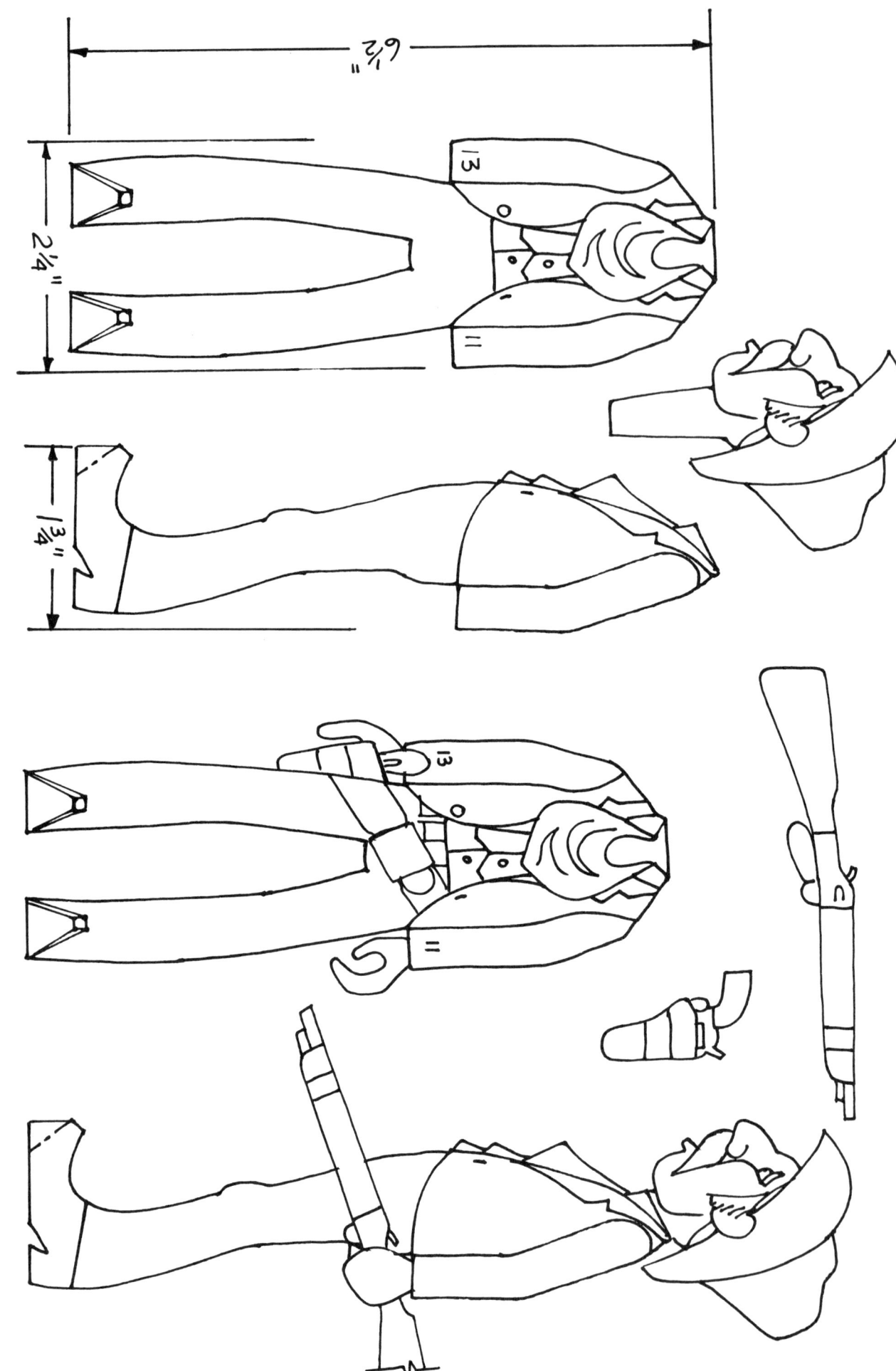

STASH McGREW

ENLARGE THIS PATTERN 133% FOR ORIGINAL SIZE.

16

REB CALLAHAN

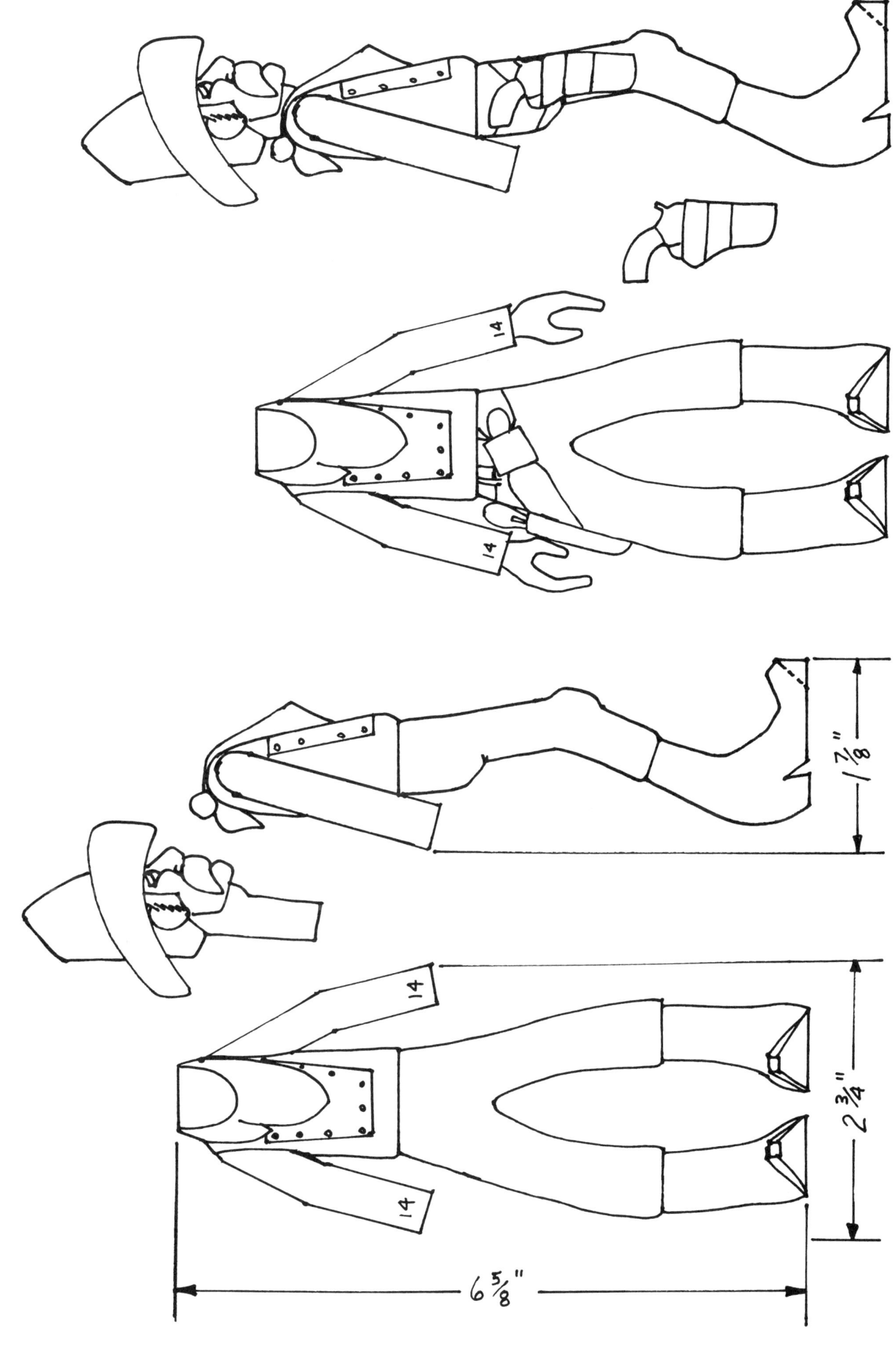

14

14

14

14

1 7/8"

2 3/4"

6 5/8"

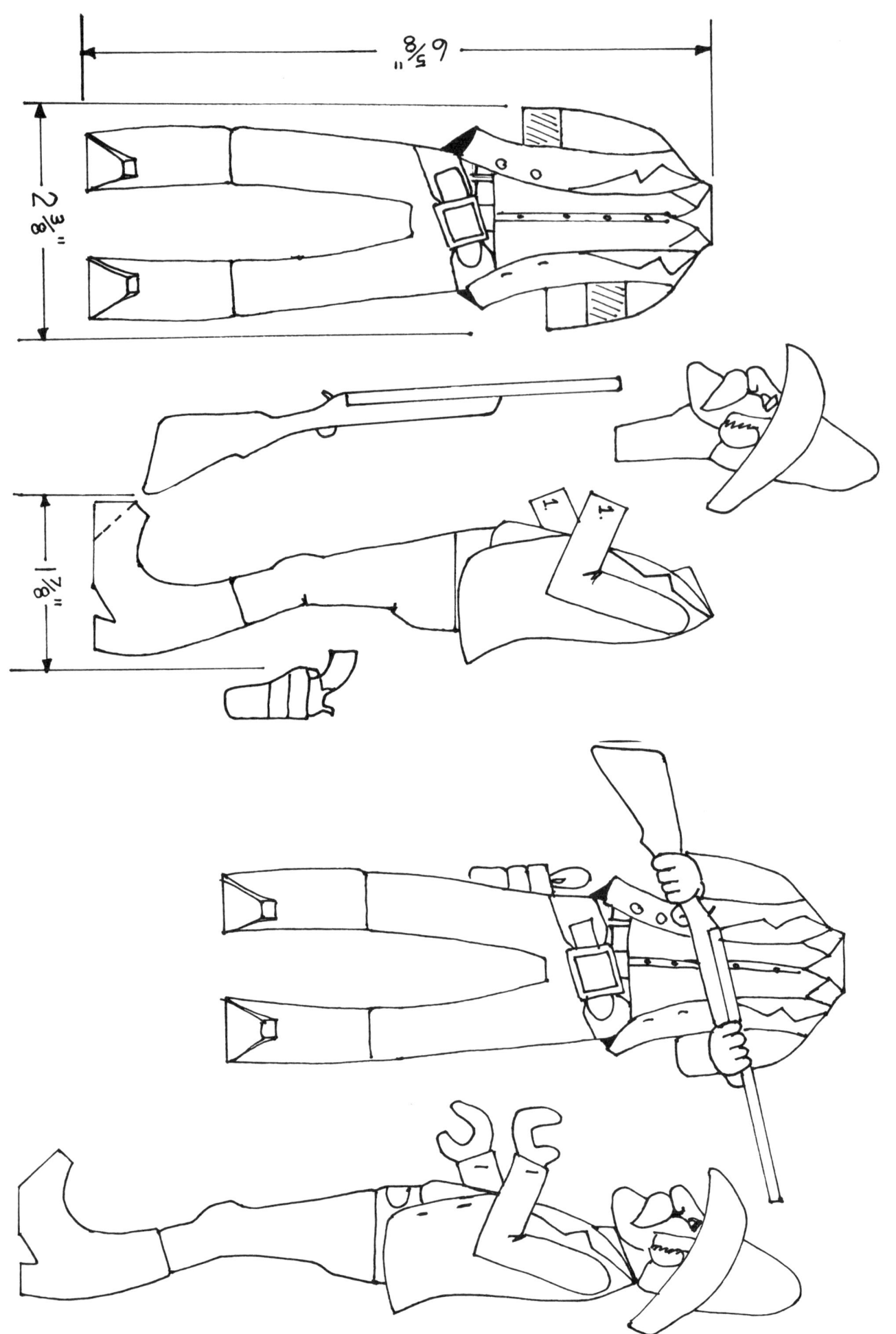

SWEDE LISIECKI

ENLARGE THIS PATTERN 133% FOR ORIGINAL SIZE.

9 5/8"

2 3/8"

1 7/8"

1.

1.

SHOOTER McCALL

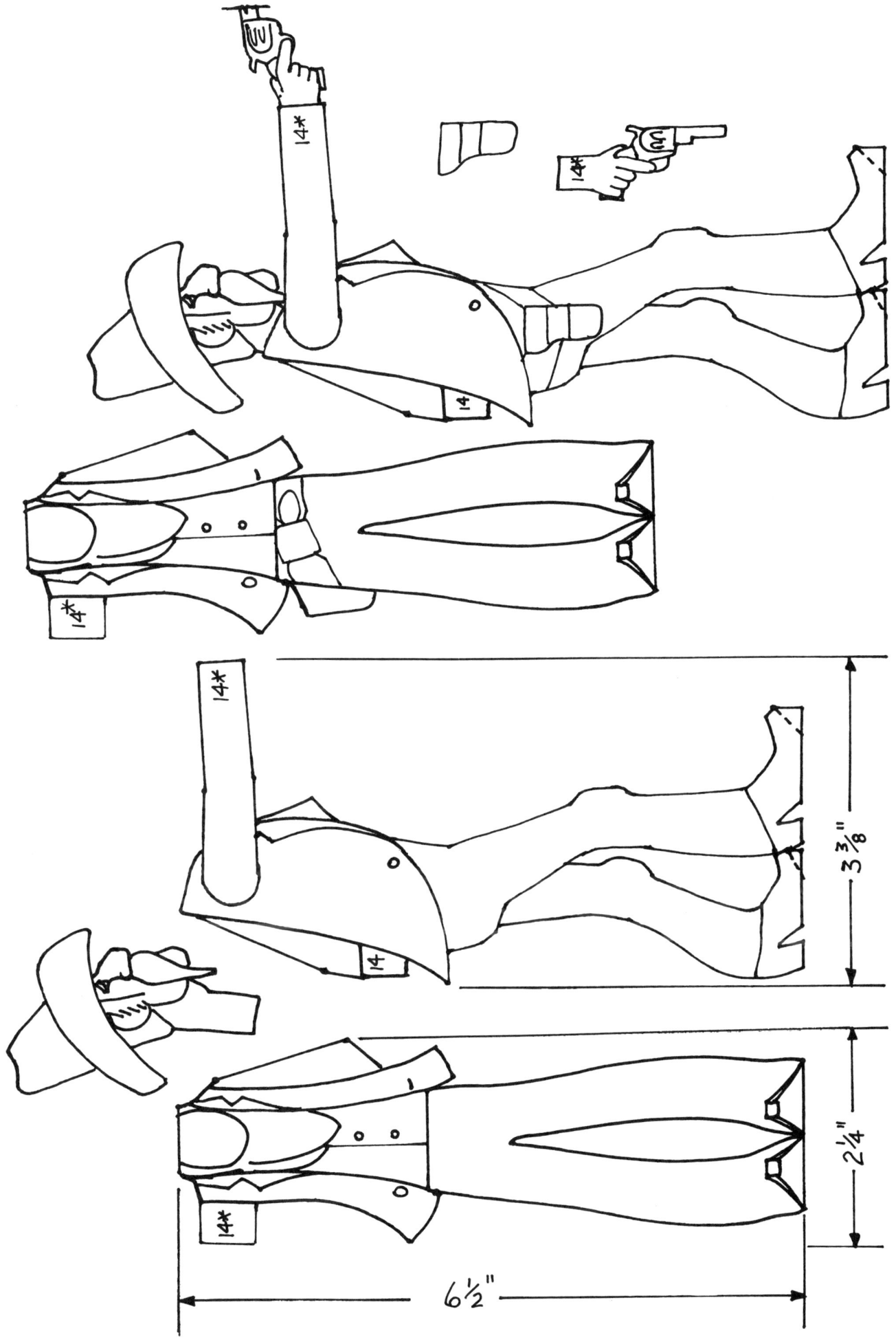

14*

14

14*

14

6½"

2¼"

3 3/8"

ENLARGE THIS PATTERN 133% FOR ORIGINAL SIZE.

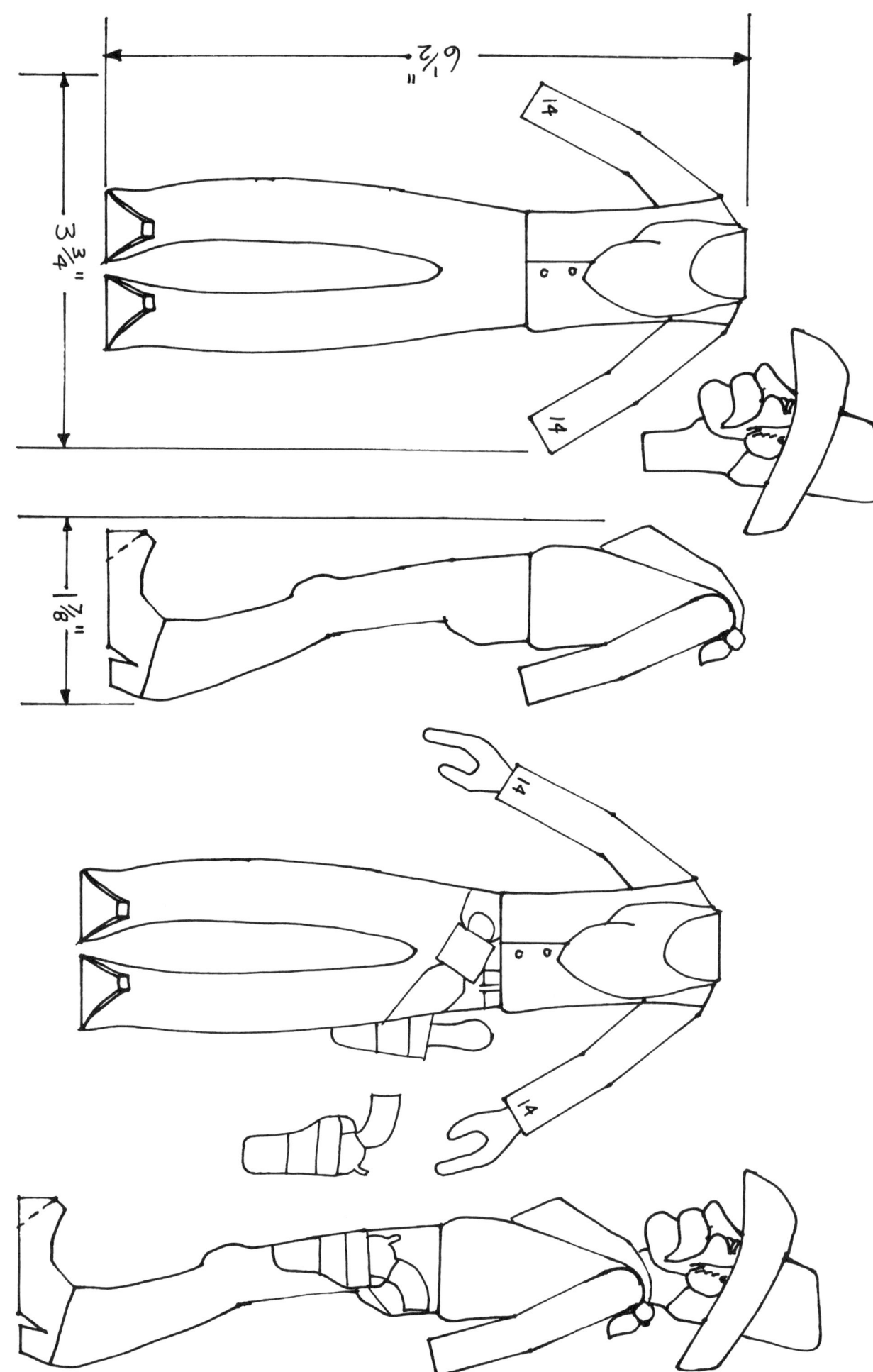

6½"

3¾"

14

14

1⅞"

6½"

14

14

CHEROKEE JIM COLLINS

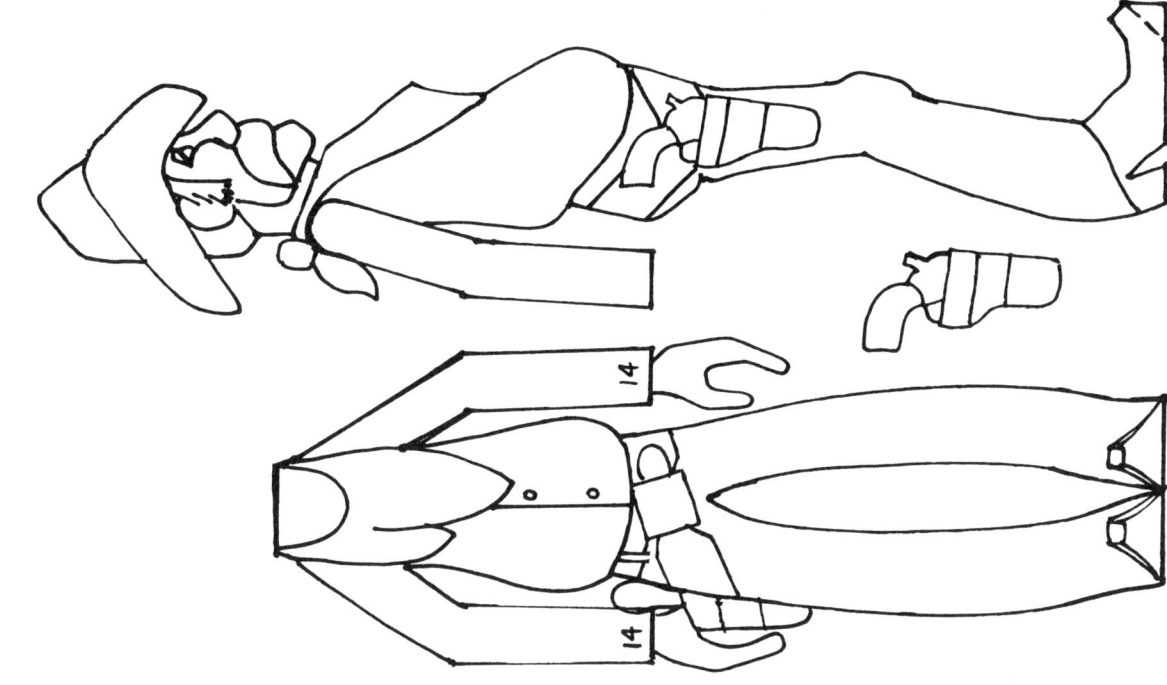

14

14

14

14

2⅛"

2¼"

6⅜"

21

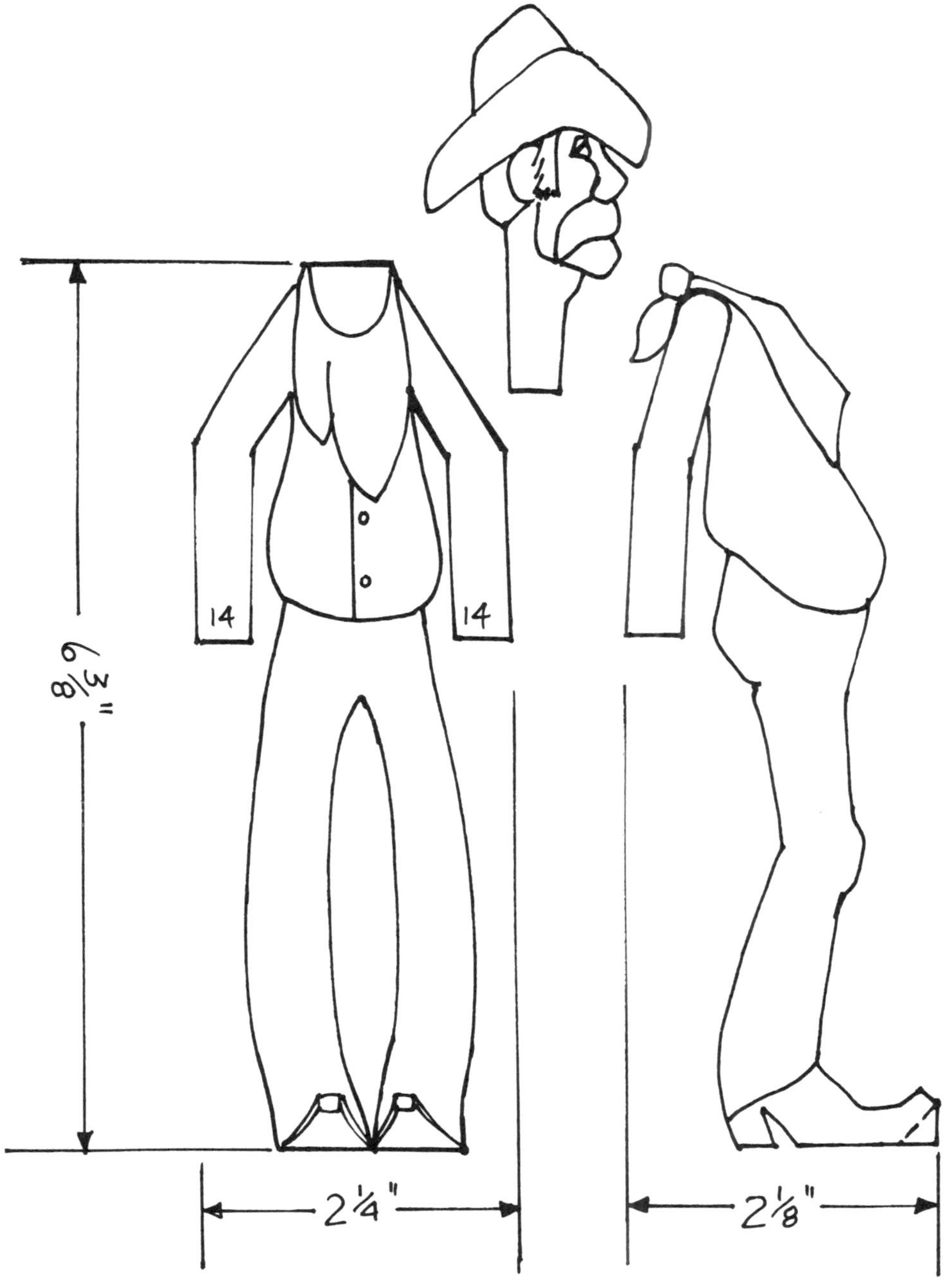

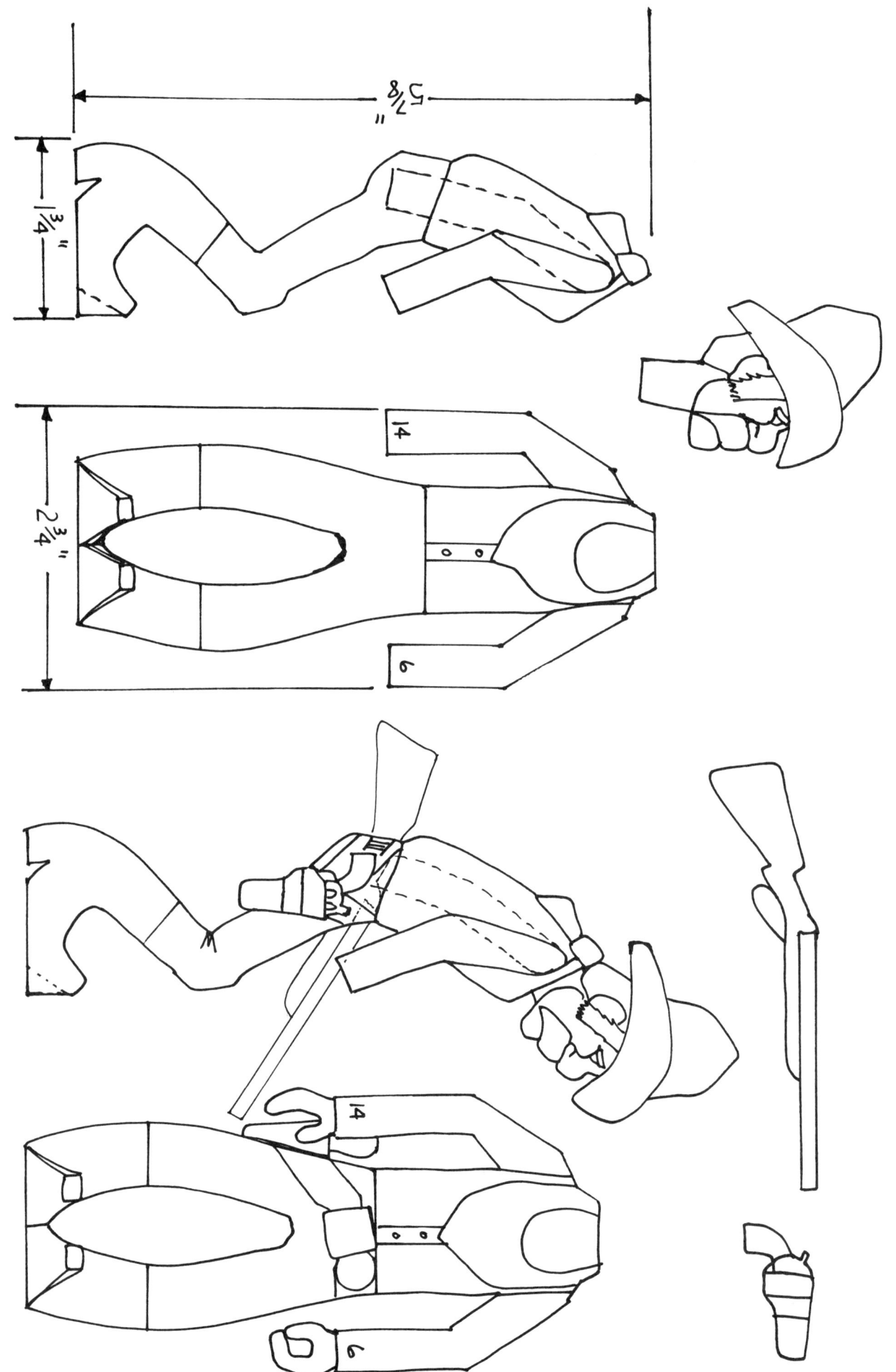

5 7/8"

1 3/4"

2 3/4"

14

6

14

6

ENLARGE THIS PATTERN 133% FOR ORIGINAL SIZE.

J. W. COOPER

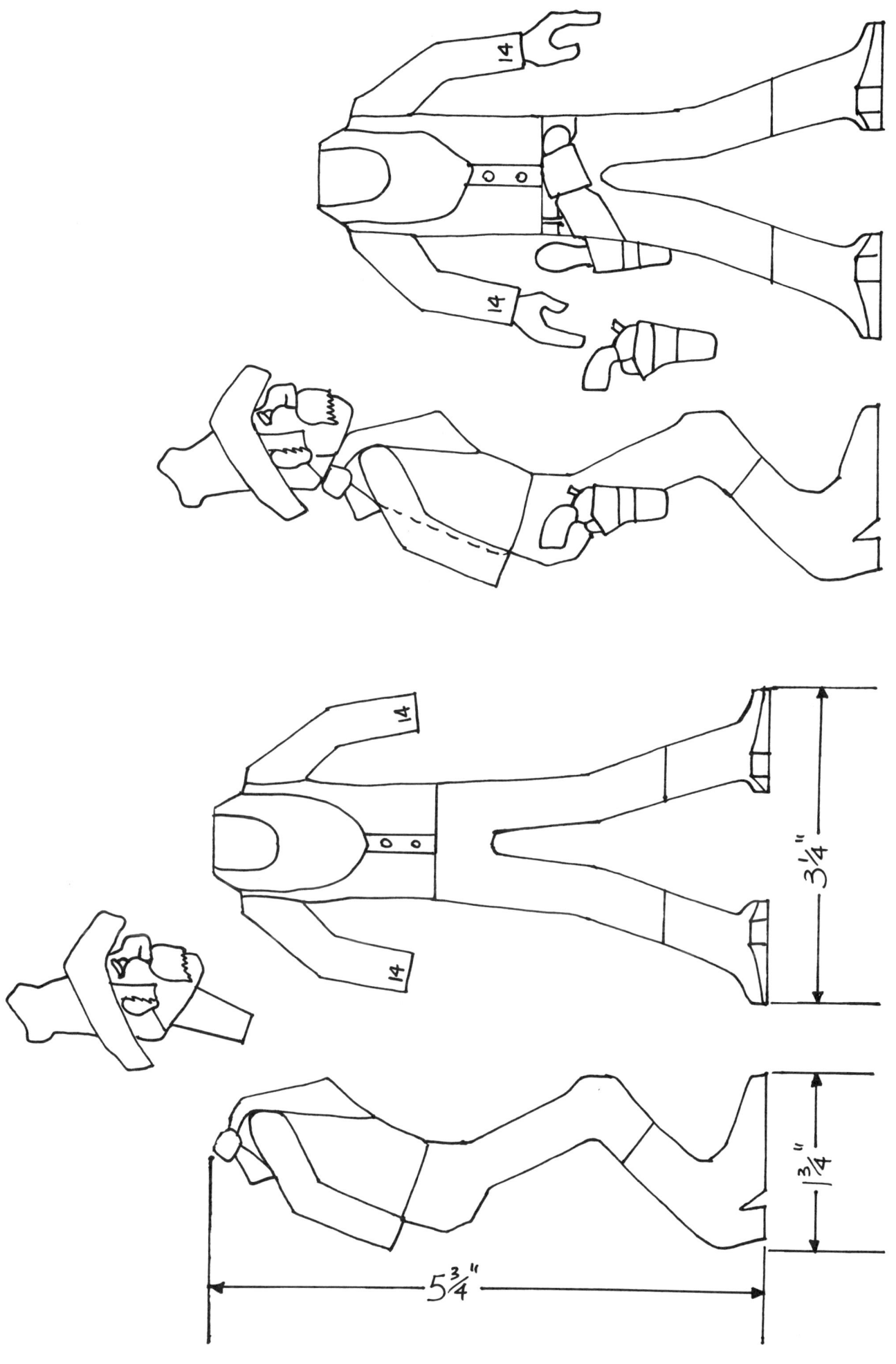

ENLARGE THIS PATTERN 133% FOR ORIGINAL SIZE.

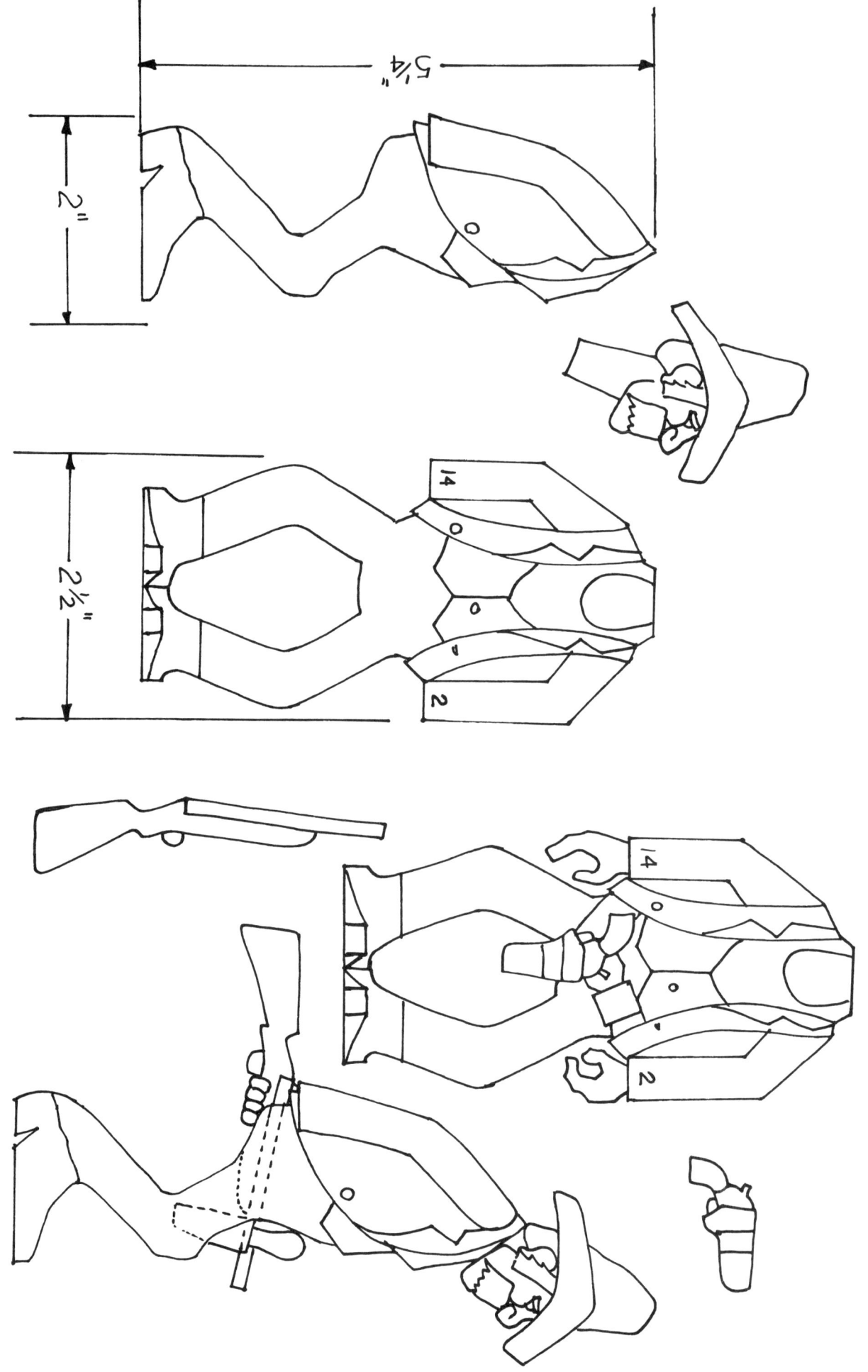

MEAN JOE SANFORD

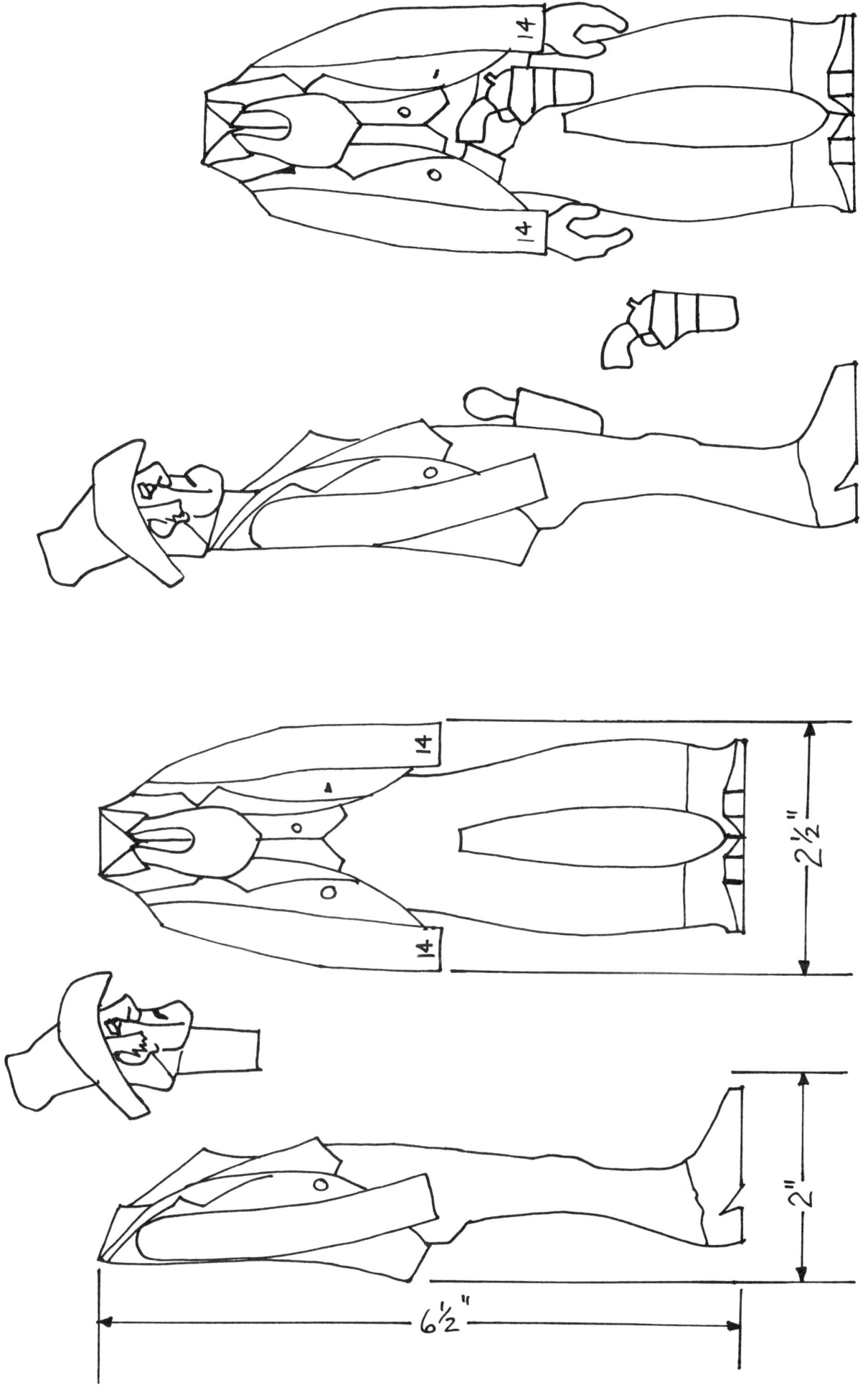

2½"

2"

6½"

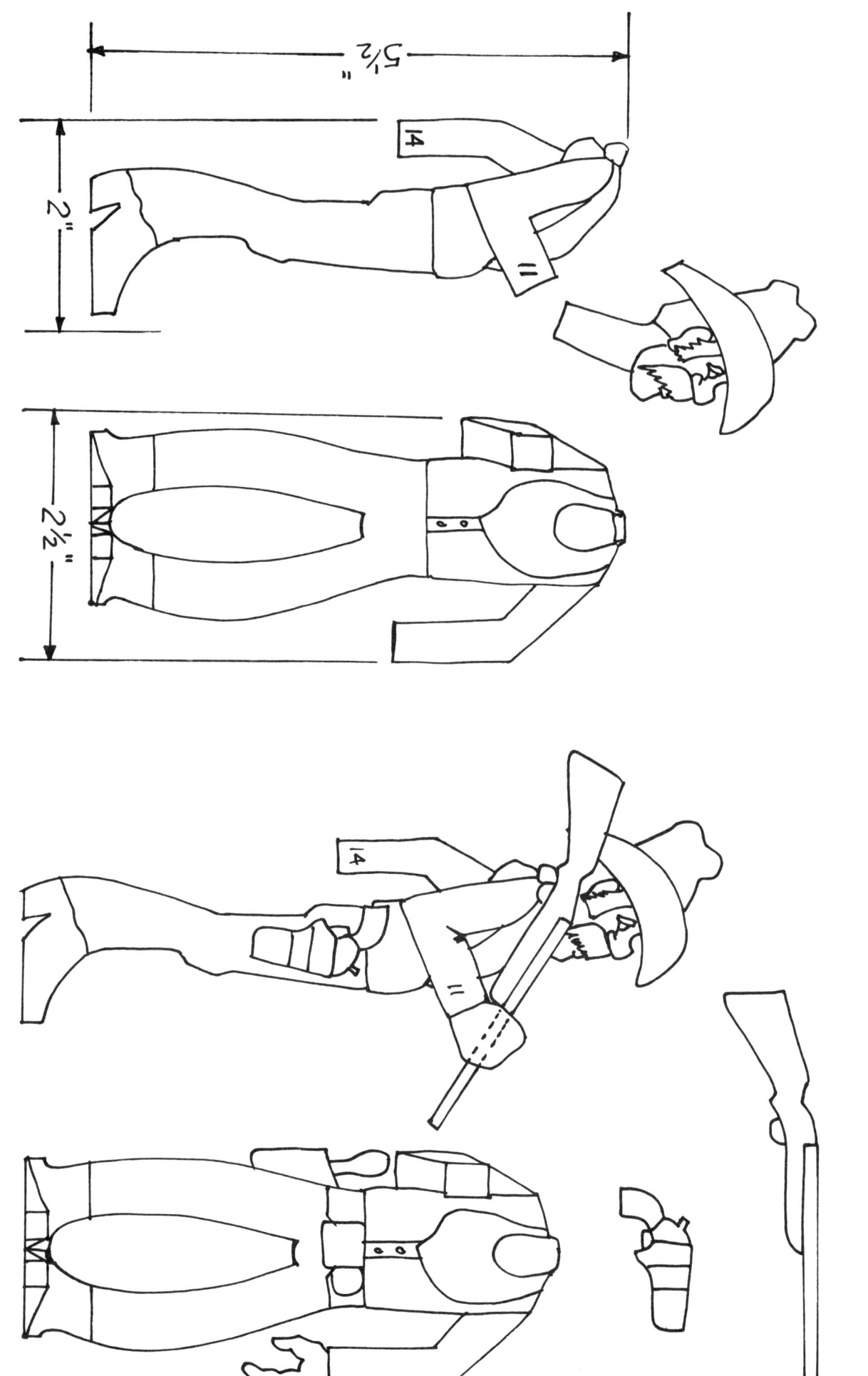

ENLARGE THIS PATTERN 133% FOR ORIGINAL SIZE.

LOUIE DREW

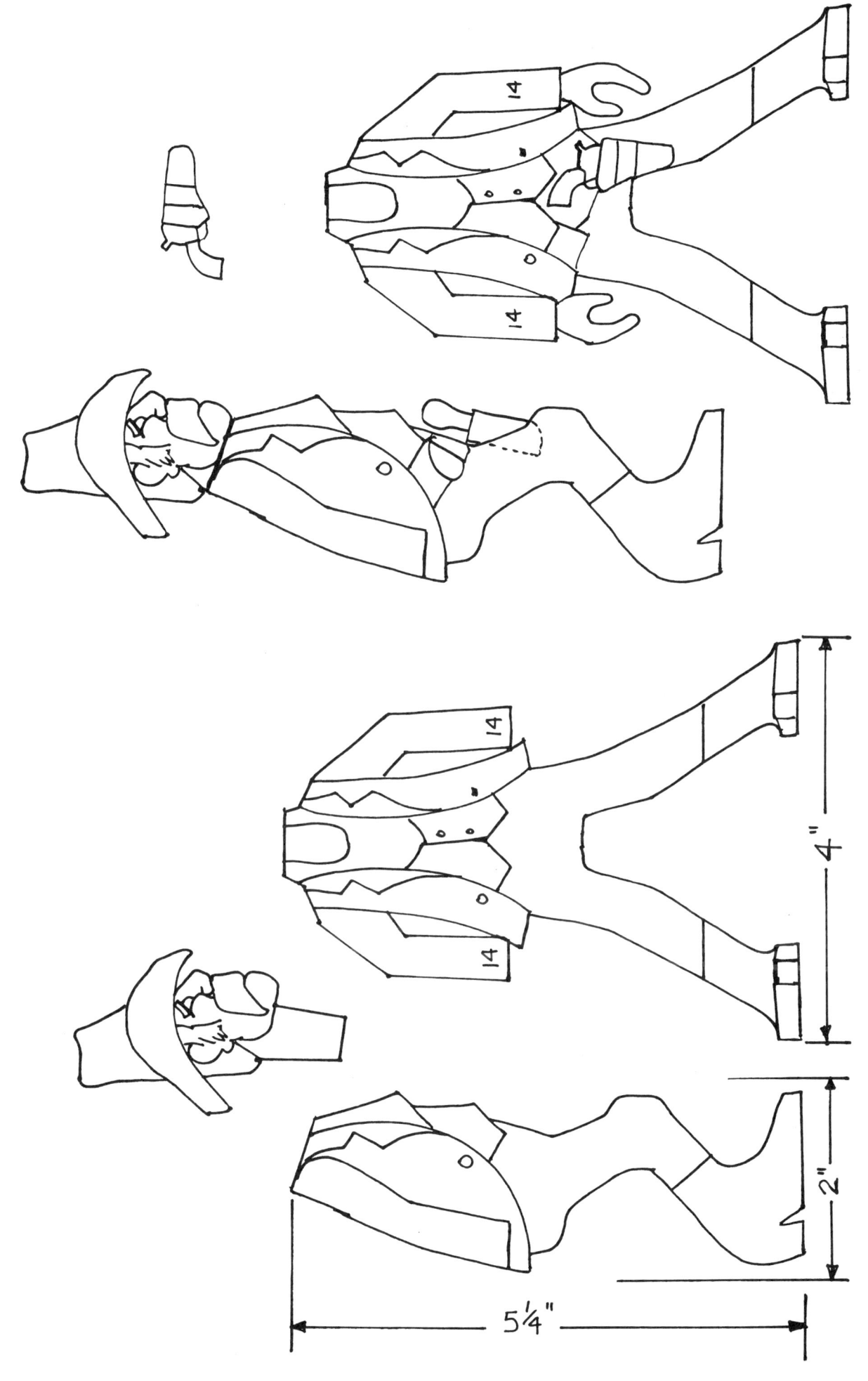

14

14

14

14

4"

2"

5¼"

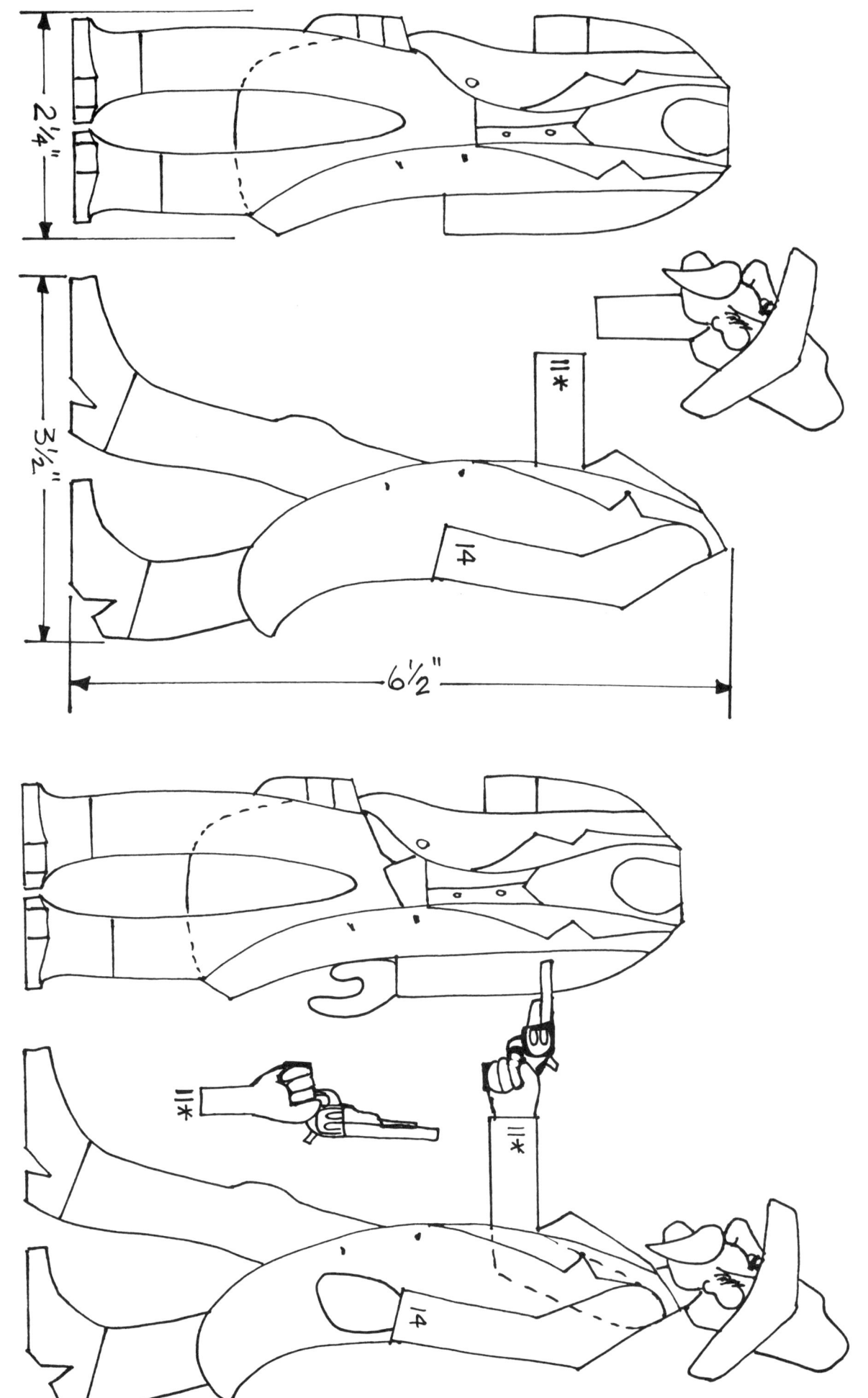

ENLARGE THIS PATTERN 133% FOR ORIGINAL SIZE.

DURANGO BOB

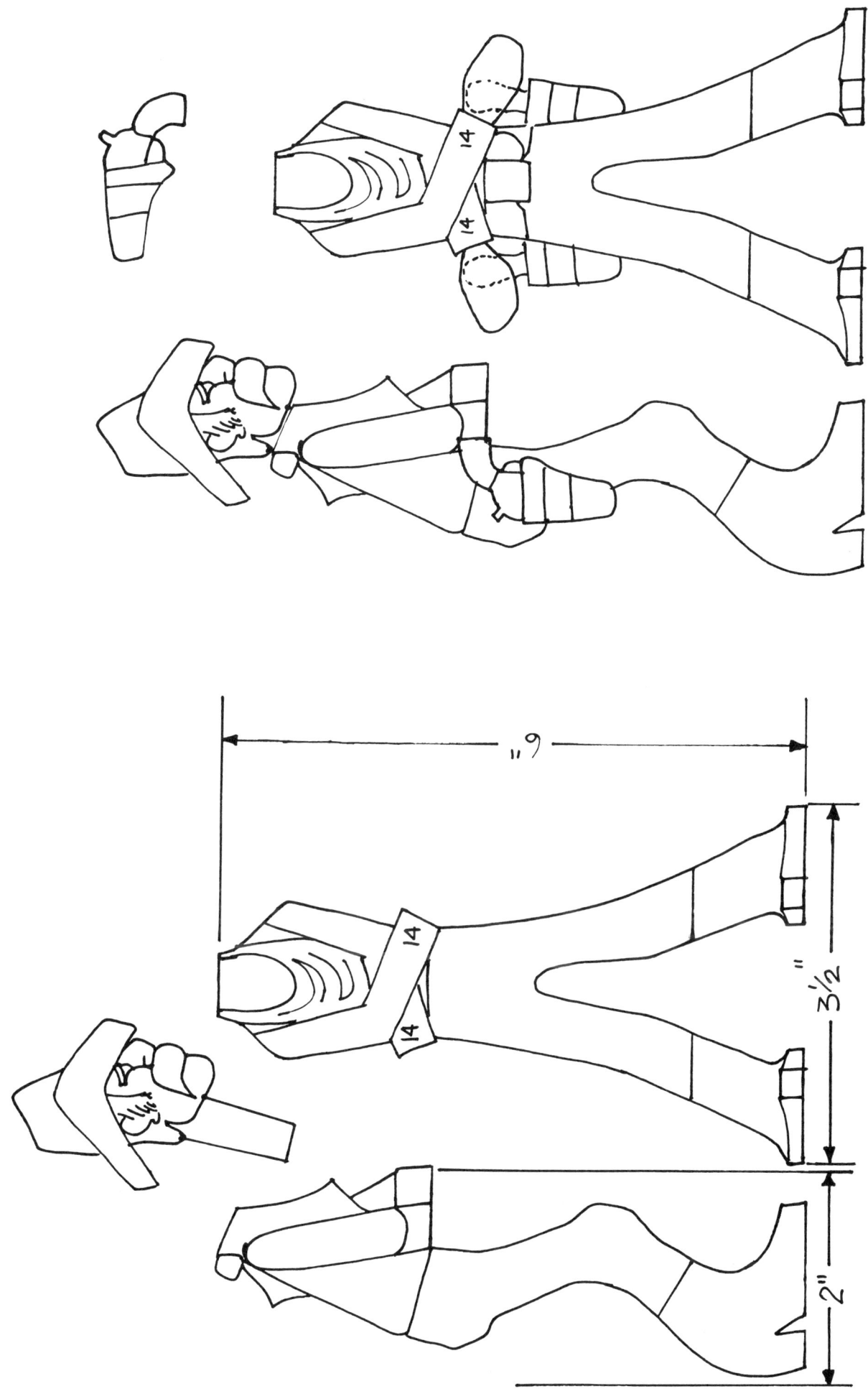

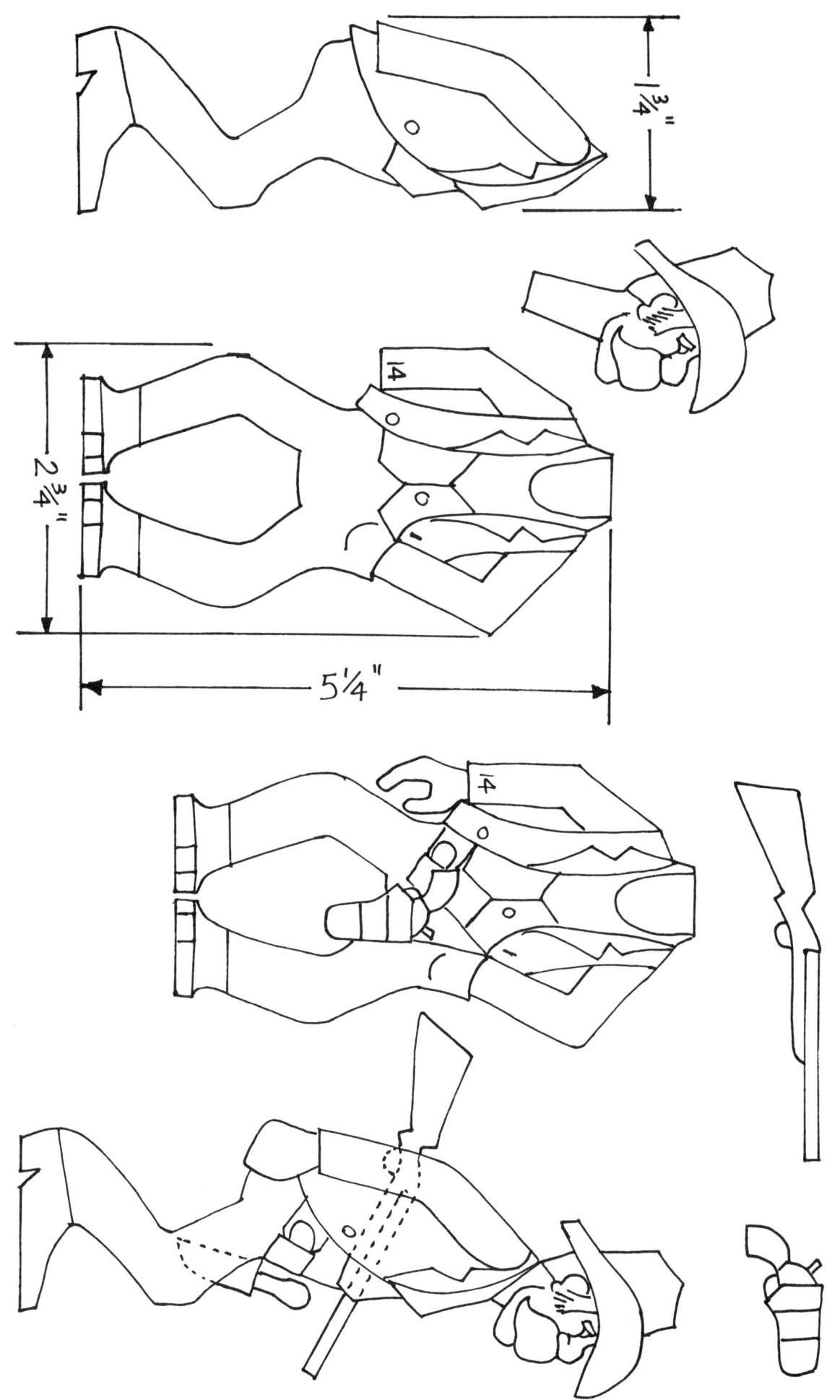

1¾"

2¾"

5¼"

14

ENLARGE THIS PATTERN 133% FOR ORIGINAL SIZE.

HENRY J. TIPPINS

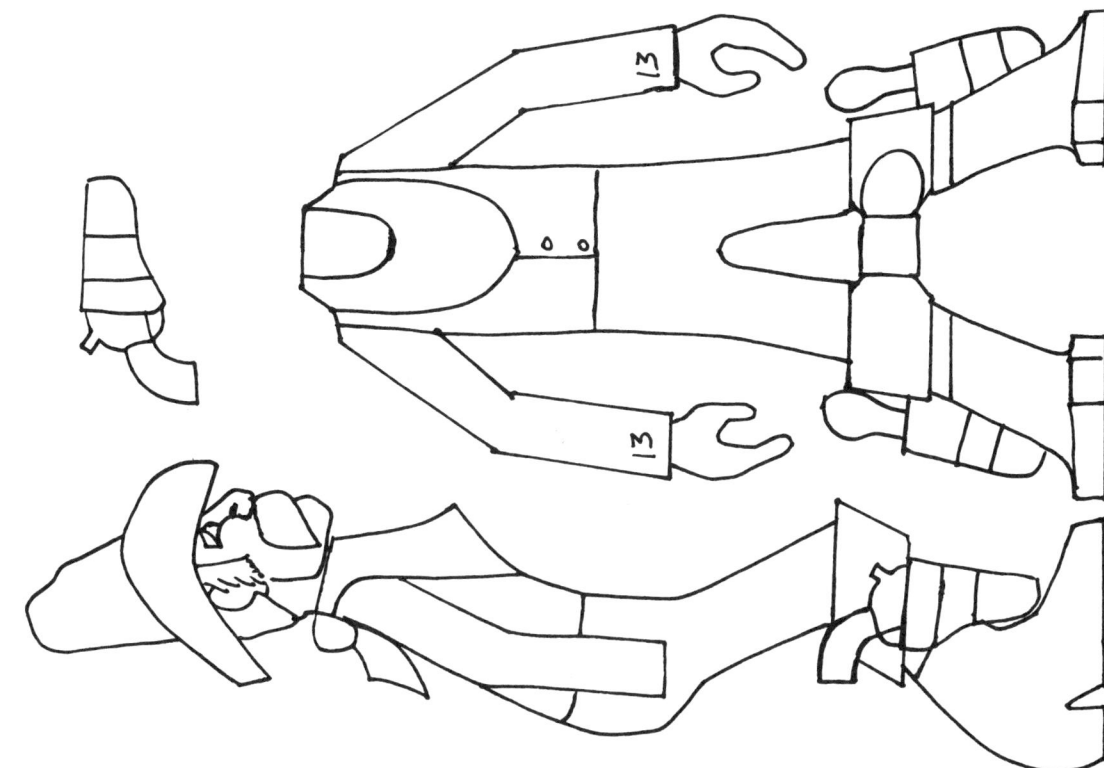

13

13

13

13

3½"

5¾"

2"

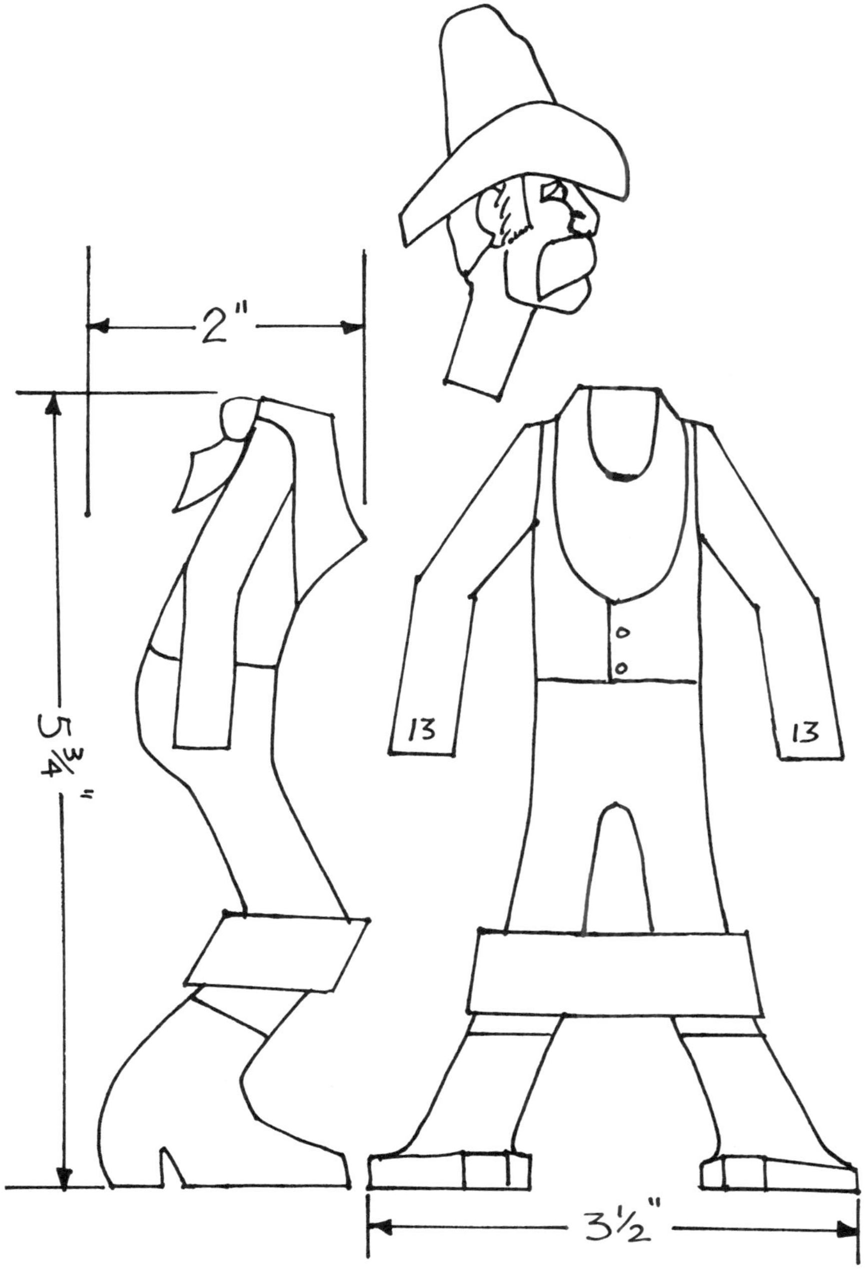

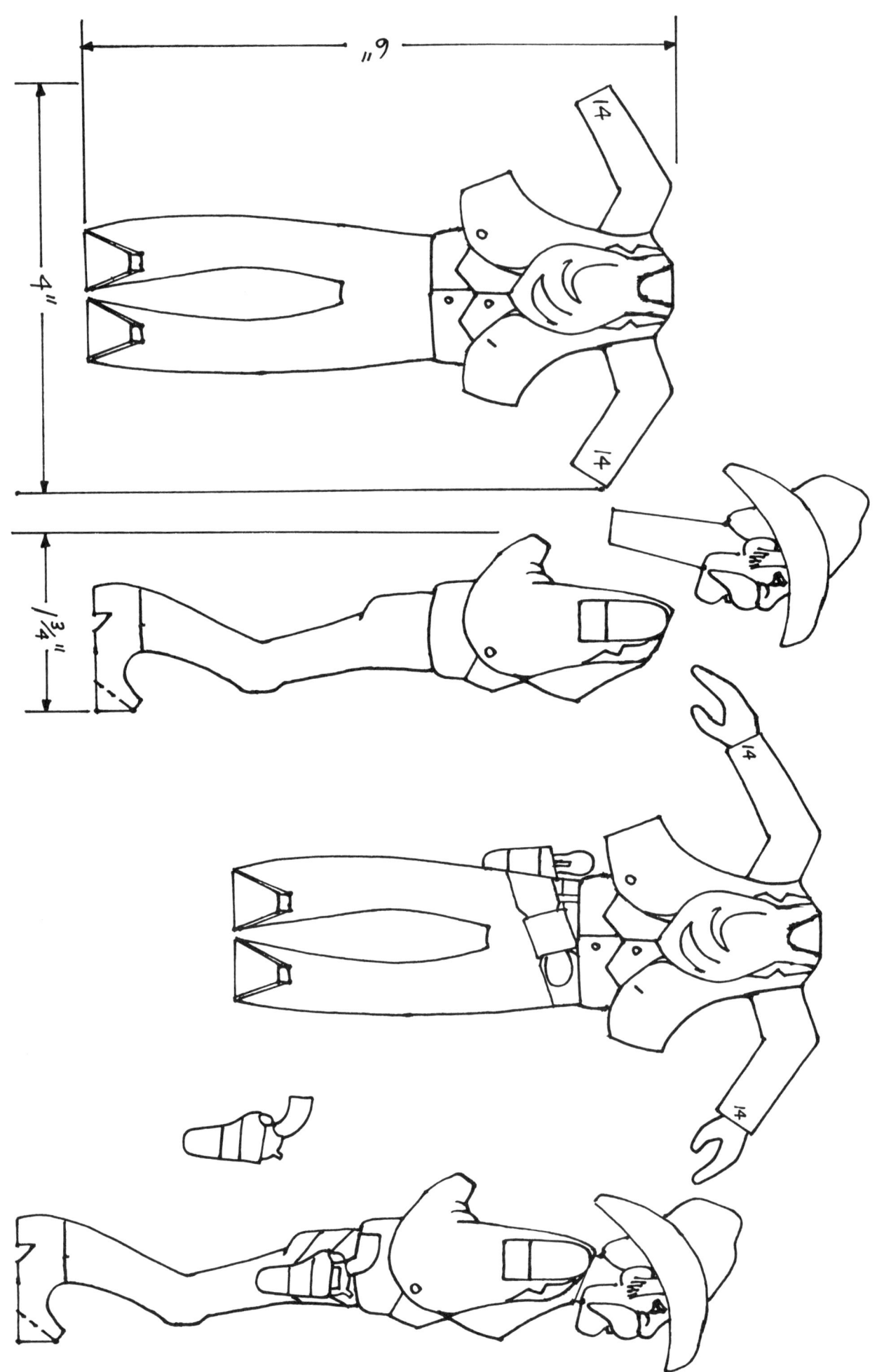

ENLARGE THIS PATTERN 133% FOR ORIGINAL SIZE.

9"

4"

3/4"

THE CARVING PROJECT

For this project, we are going to carve one of my gunfighter caricatures. We will do it in four phases, much the same way as I do when I am carving figures and caricatures. We will carve the head first. This is the **most** important part of a character carving, because it determines the carving's personality.

The body, hands and accessories just complement the head and face. After the head is carved, we will carve the body. Then, we will carve the hands. This step will give you a chance to use my "magic" hand template. I will discuss the hand template in more detail during that section of the carving project. Finally, we will carve the pistol. If you're ready, let's get started.

CARVING THE HEAD

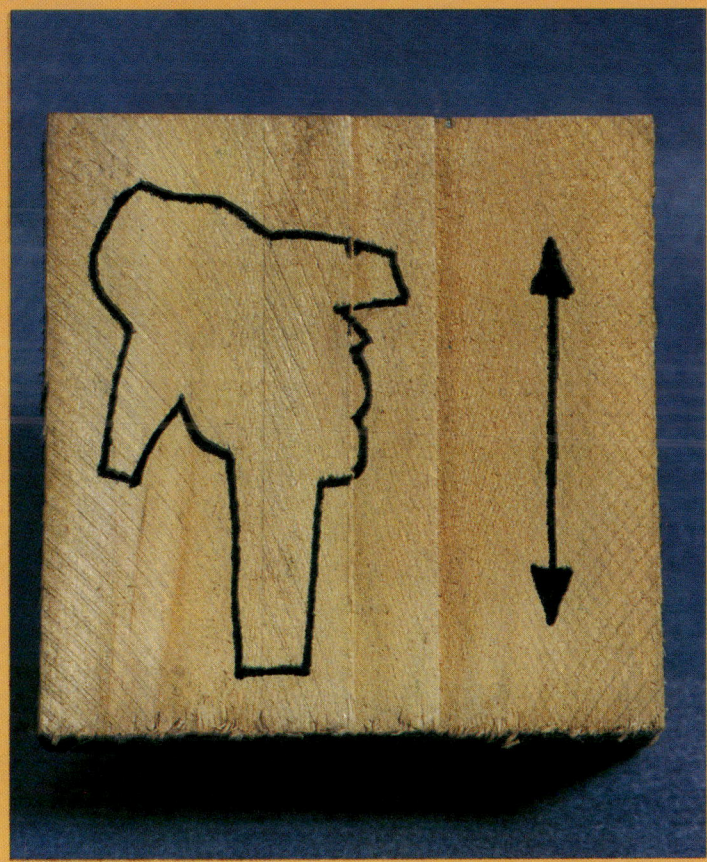

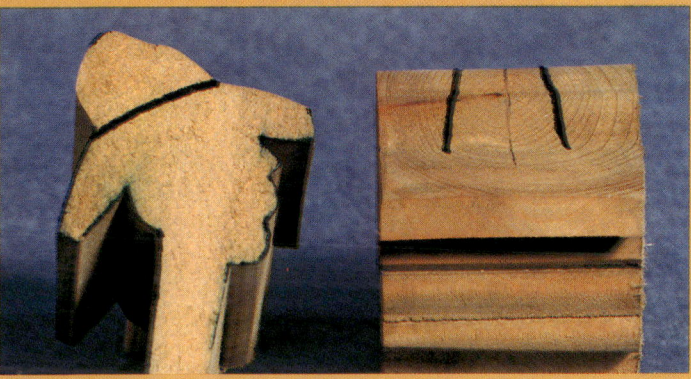

Sketch in the side view of the hat brim, and the front view of the crown, as shown by the heavy dark lines in the photo. This is an area you can experiment with on future carvings. The width of the crown from left to right will determine the width of the face and hair, as you will see in a later step.

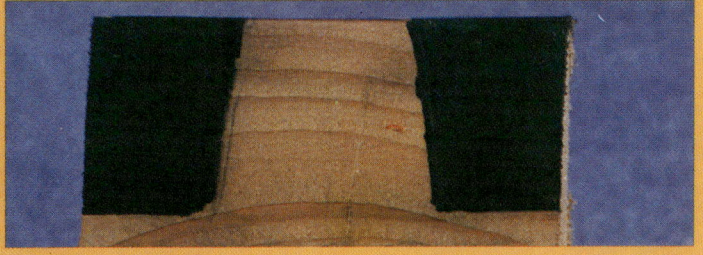

Transfer the head pattern to the wood and saw it out, using a bandsaw, coping saw, or other means. Pay close attention to the direction of the wood grain in the photo. You want the grain to run vertically through the head. This will make carving easier, and will give the head maximum strength.

In this front view, you can see where I have darkened the wood I want to remove, in order to establish the rough shape of the crown. **I will use this darkened wood method, when possible, in all future steps of the carving project, to help you see what wood is to be removed.**

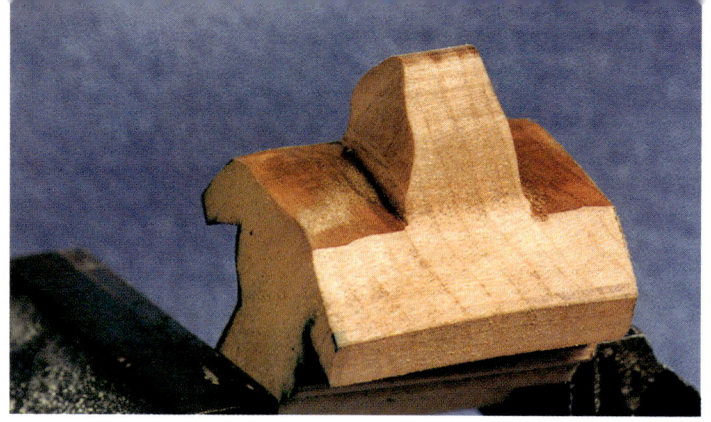

Now, clamp the head securely in a vise. Clamp the neck area, so the hat will be clear for you to work on. Using a coping saw, cut in *horizontally* from the sides, along the **top** of the brim, until you reach the vertical lines you drew earlier for the crown width. Next, saw *down* from the top, following the vertical lines, until you connect with the horizontal cuts. The section of wood should fall away, leaving the crown and upper brim roughly shaped and ready for some preliminary carving.

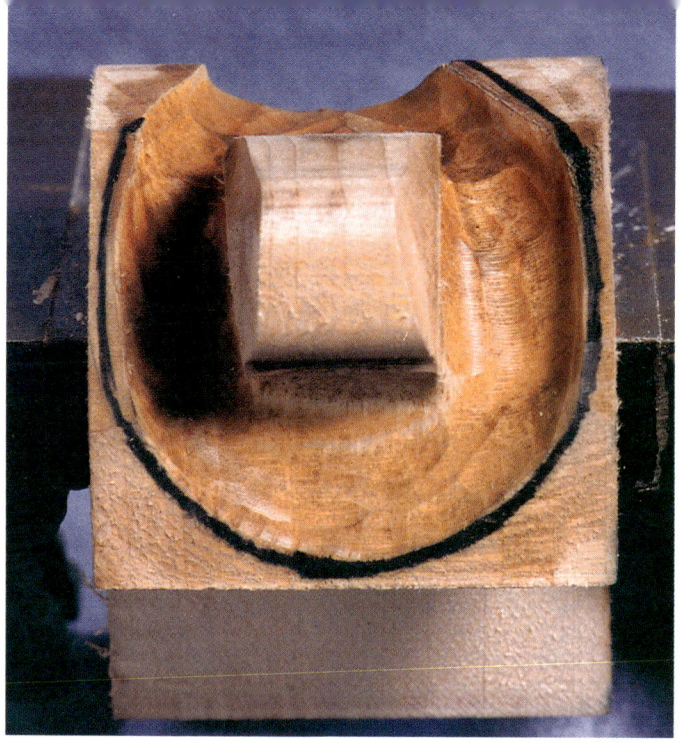

About halfway around, you may have noticed the wood grain starting to "fight" you. At this point, turn the head around in the vise. Go to the front center of the **upper** side of the brim, and start working toward the rear of the brim, until you have cut a channel all the way around the crown.

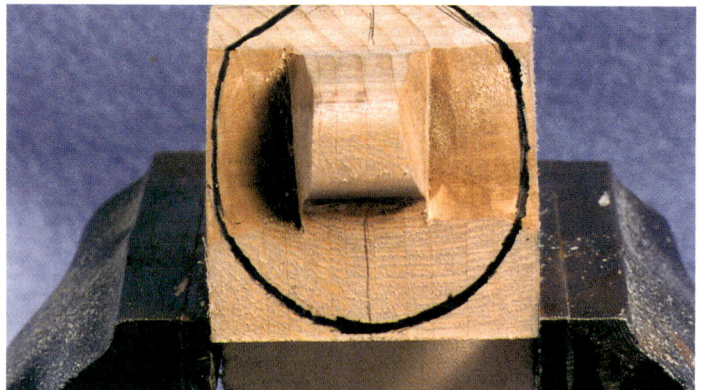

Viewing the head from the top, sketch the **outside** edges of the brim. The shape of the brim is up to you. Sometimes I make it a round shape, and other times I bring it to a point in front and rounded in the back, as I am doing for this project.

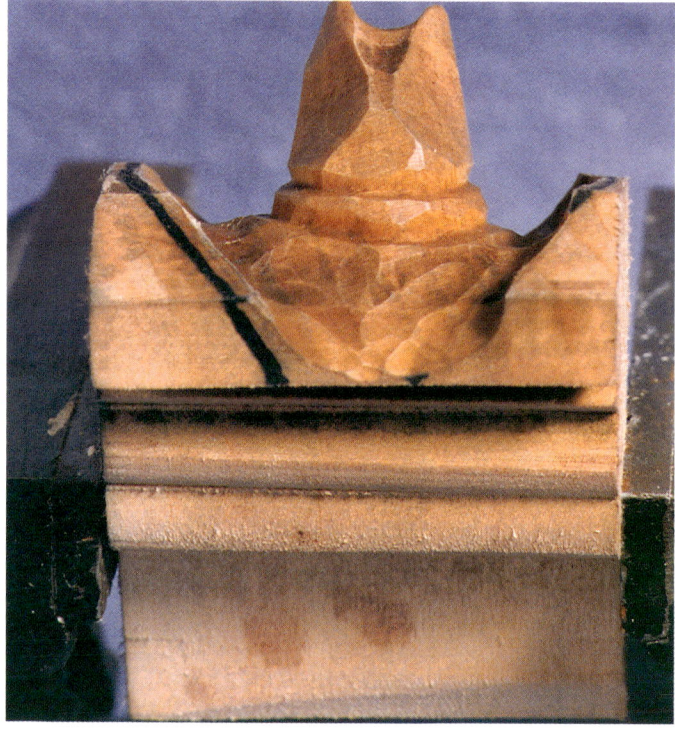

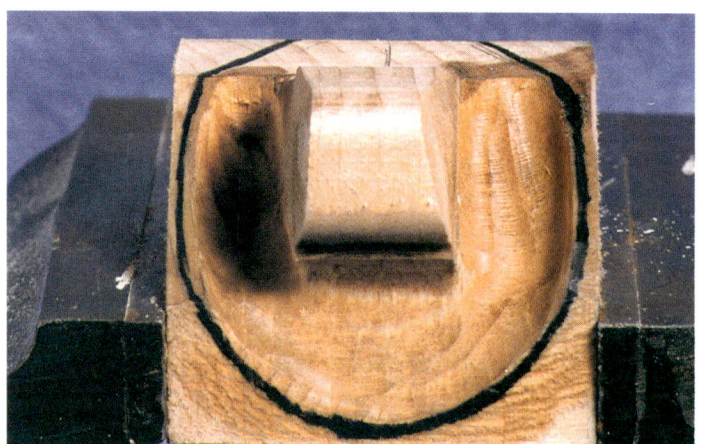

Starting from the rear center of the **upper** side of the brim, use a **#10 6mm "U" gouge** to cut a "U" shaped channel in the brim. The channel should follow the shape of the brim you outlined in the previous step. Don't press too hard, or go too deep for now. Work the channel forward until you get about halfway around each side of the crown.

Now, remove the head from the vise, and use your knife to remove all the sharp edges from the crown. Cut from the bottom of the crown toward the top on the two front edges, and from the top down toward the brim on the two back edges. You want to achieve a fairly rounded shape for the crown, but it doesn't have to be totally smooth. Leaving some of the knife cuts and facets in the wood will give the hat some "character". As an option, you also may want to use a small gouge such as a **3mm #41 "V" gouge** to go around the base of the crown and cut in a hatband, as I did here.

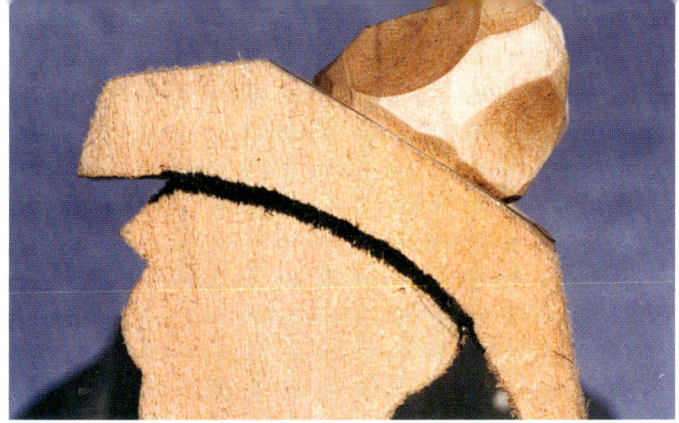

Next, draw a line as shown, on the side of the head, to define where the bottom of the hat will rest on the head.

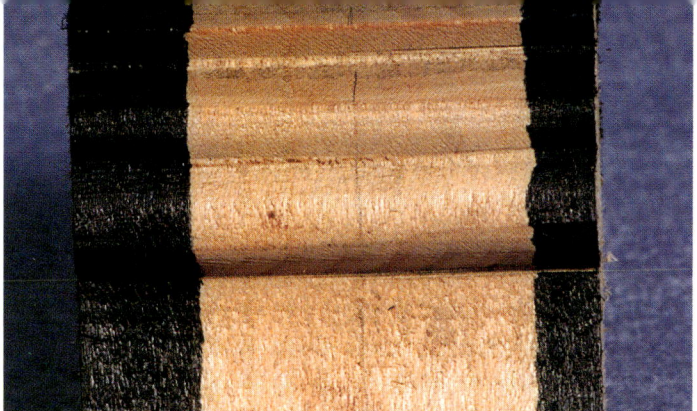

Next, lay the head on its **back** and saw away the darkened areas.

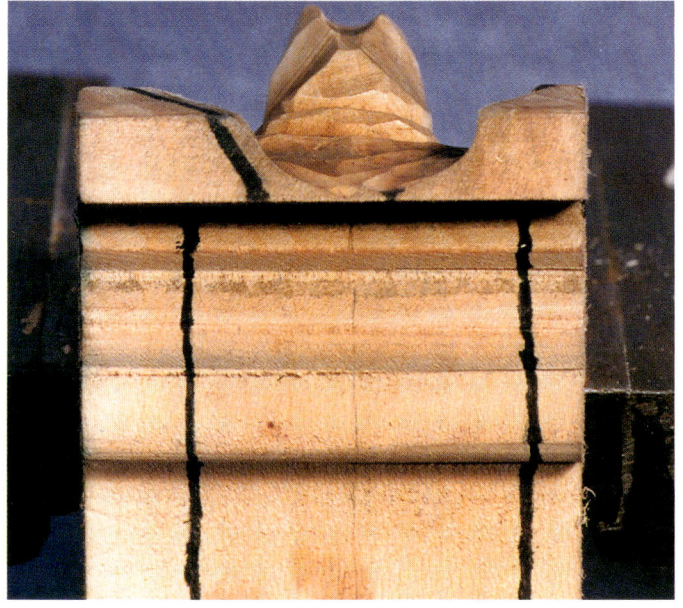

With the head facing you, draw two reference lines to roughly define the outer edges of the hair and ears. These lines will be governed by how wide you made the crown earlier. We are leaving the head wide enough so we can give our gunfighter a nice set of ears.

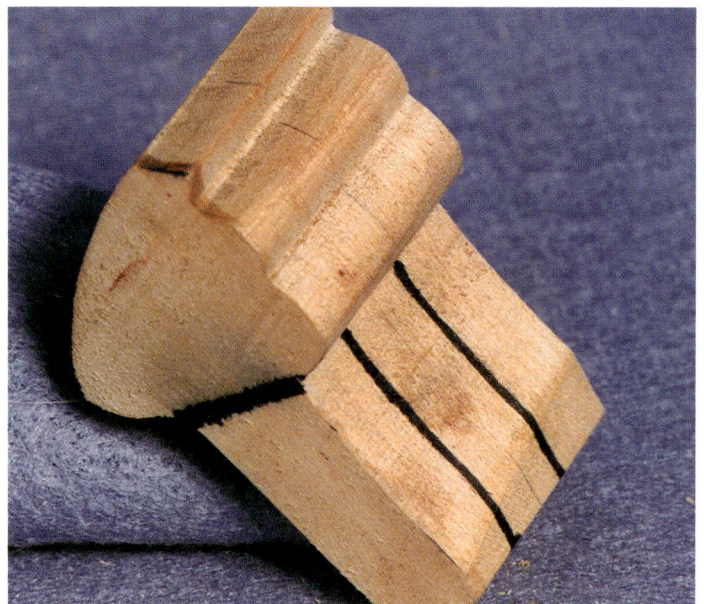

To establish the rough neck size, sketch in the front and side neck lines, as shown.

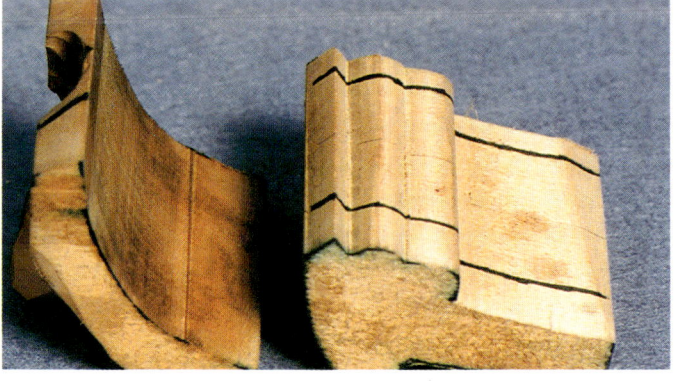

We now want to separate the hat from the head, so we can carve the face, ears, hair and neck **easily**. (This trick works on any carving wearing a hat). Lay the head on its **side** and saw along the line you drew earlier. After separating the two pieces, rub a small amount of wood glue into the **top** of the head, and **bottom** of the hat. This will seal the wood and will make a better joint when we glue the pieces back together later.

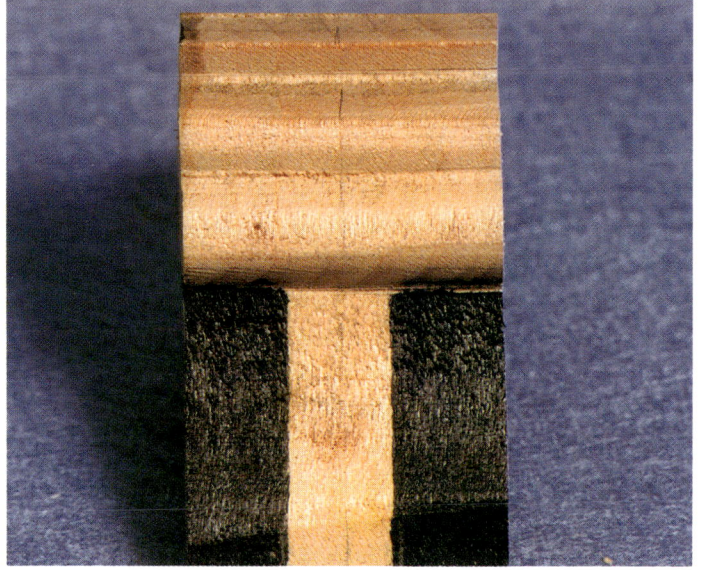

Use your coping saw to remove the darkened sections of wood, the same way as you removed the sections of wood to form the crown of the hat.

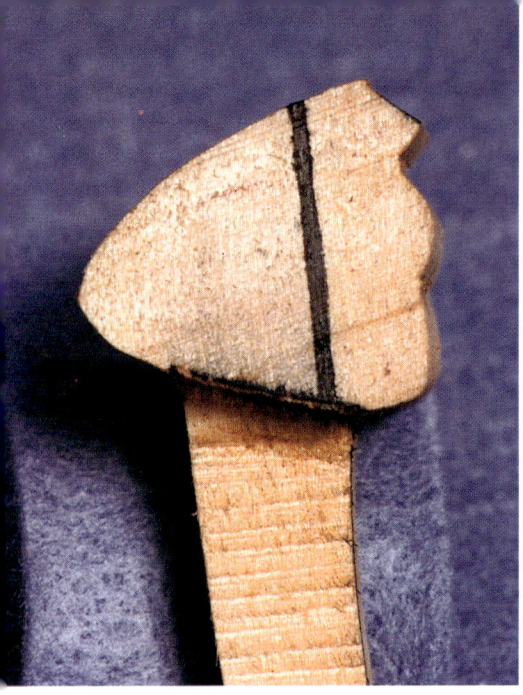
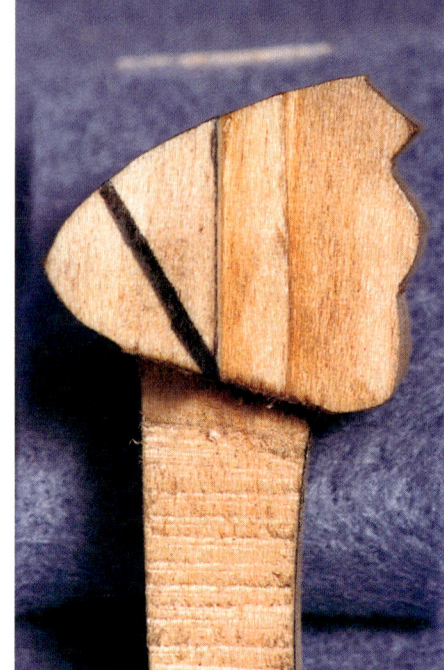
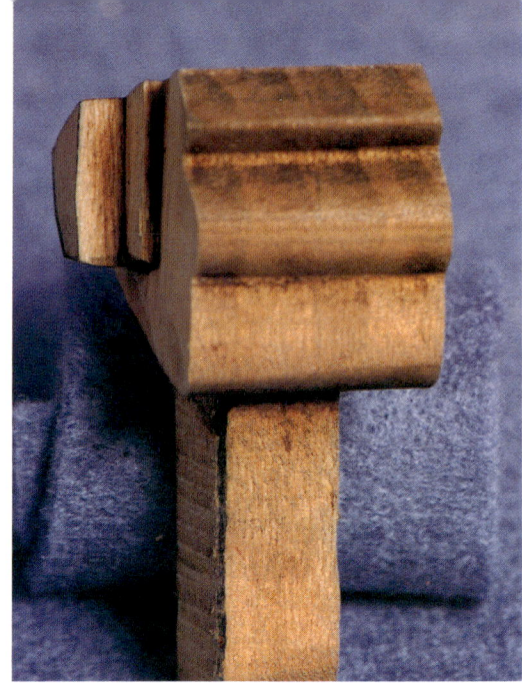

Now draw a **vertical** line down the side of the head, as shown. (Do this on both sides of the head, slightly forward of the middle of the head). This will define the front edge of the sideburns. Using the tip of your knife, incise along this line about 1/8" deep. Next, shave in from the **front** of the head, until the piece of wood comes free. Repeat this until you have removed a piece of wood approximately 1/4" thick from both sides of the face. (This doesn't have to be exact. The deeper you cut, the more the ears will protrude and the narrower the face will be).

Starting from the bottom rear corner of the sideburn, draw a line upward to the top of the head, so that a triangle is formed. The wider you make the triangle, the larger the finished ear will be. Repeat for the other side of the face.

I like to make the top of the ears even with the top of the head so the hat will rest nicely on top of them, and the bottom of the ears and sideburns about even with the bottom of the nose. You can vary this, depending on how much of a caricature you want your gunfighter to be. Make a **horizontal** cut to define the bottom of the ears and sideburns, and remove the excess wood.

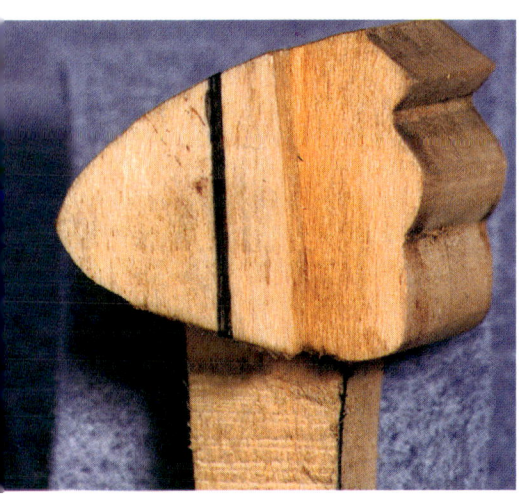
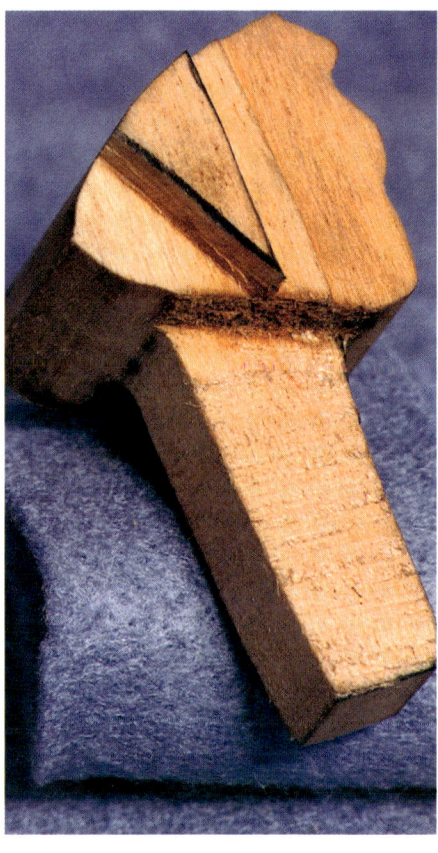
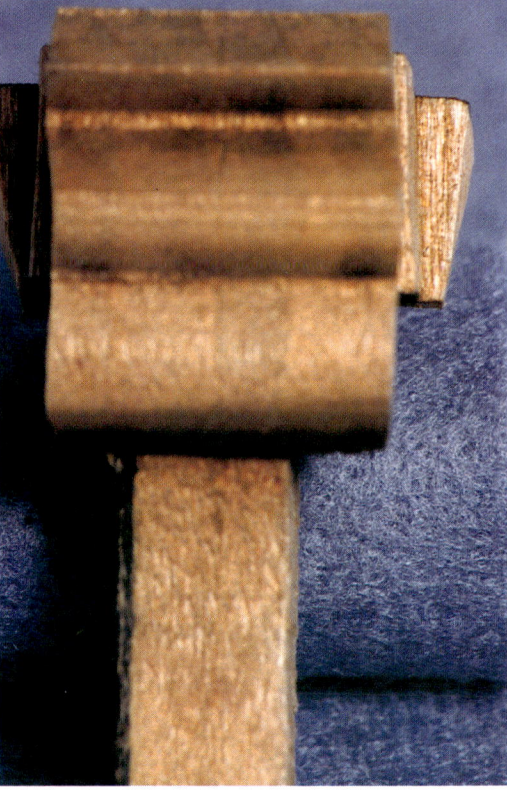

Draw a <u>vertical</u> line up the side of the head, about 1/8" behind the front edge of the sideburn. Incise this line and shave back toward it from the front of the head. Repeat this incising and shaving, until the sideburns are about 1/16" thick. Again, this doesn't have to be exact. You can leave the sideburns thicker, if you so desire. The more you shave the sideburns down, the more the ears will protrude. Do this on each side of the head.

Now take your knife and incise along the back edge of the triangle. Shave toward the back edge with your knife and remove enough wood to make the ear stand out from the head in back. Repeat as desired until the ear stands out like you want it to.

Starting at the **top** of the ear outline, shave downward, so the ears protrude at the top of the head, and taper to be nearly flush with the sideburns at the bottom.

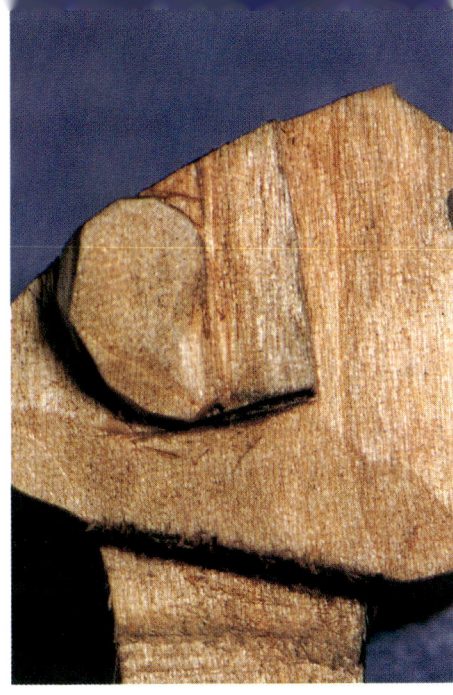

Remove the sharp corners from the front and rear of the ears. Repeat as necessary until the ears have a nice rounded shape.

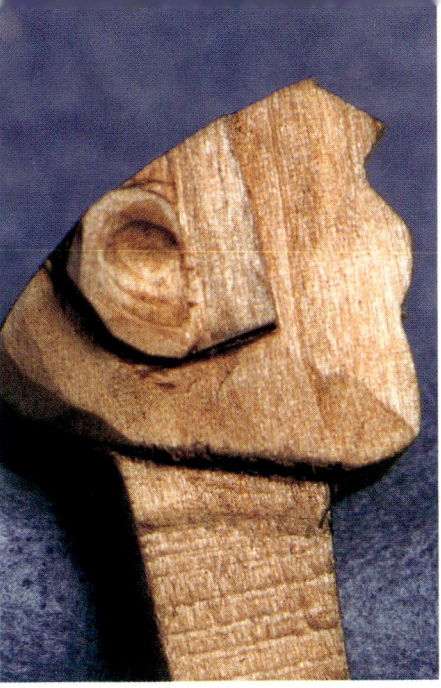

Now, use your knife to knock off the rear corners of the head. While you are here, round off the sharp edges on the back of the head, but don't carve on the neck, yet.

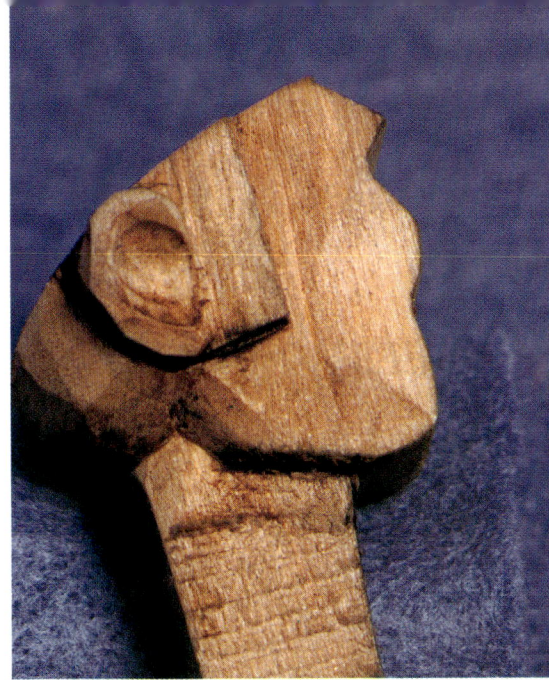

Round off the sharp hair edges you just made, and round off any remaining sharp edges on the back part of the head.

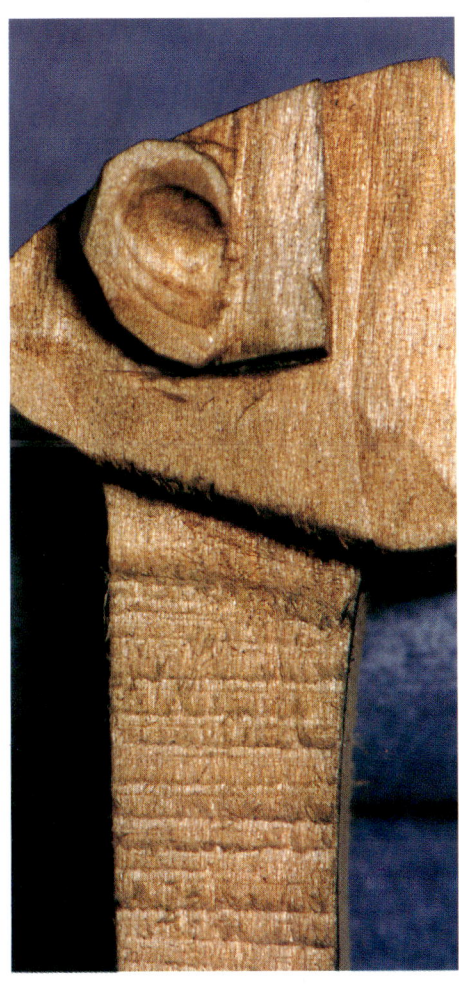

Use a **#10 3mm "U" gouge** to remove wood from the inside of the ears, cutting in from the rear edge of the ears, toward the sideburn.

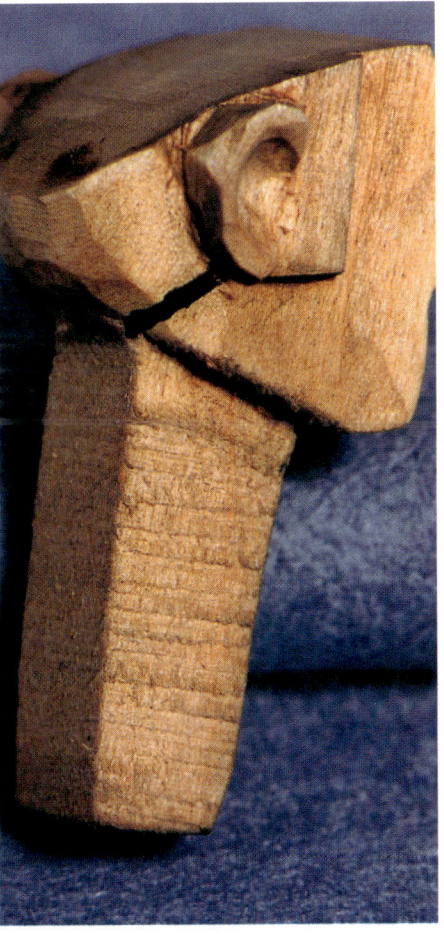

Draw a slanted line from the back of the ear to the back of the head, to define the rear hair line. Incise this line about 1/8" deep and shave up toward it from the neck.

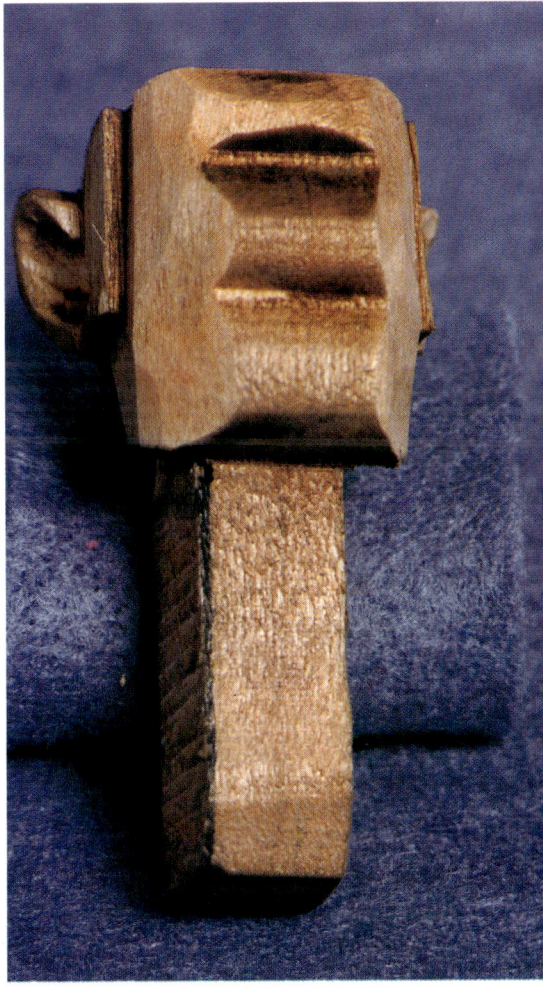

Remove the sharp corners from the front edges of the face, using your knife.

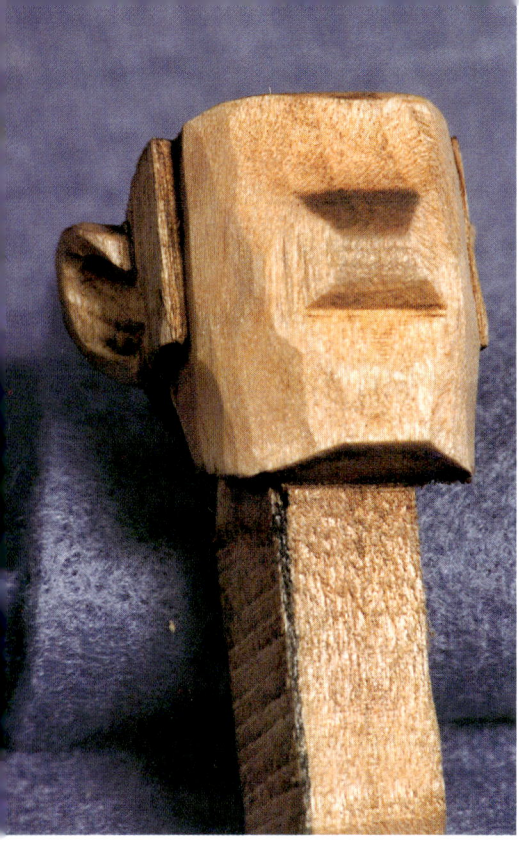

Now round off the new sharp edges you just produced. You want a fairly round face, from the outer edges of the nose, around to the sideburns.

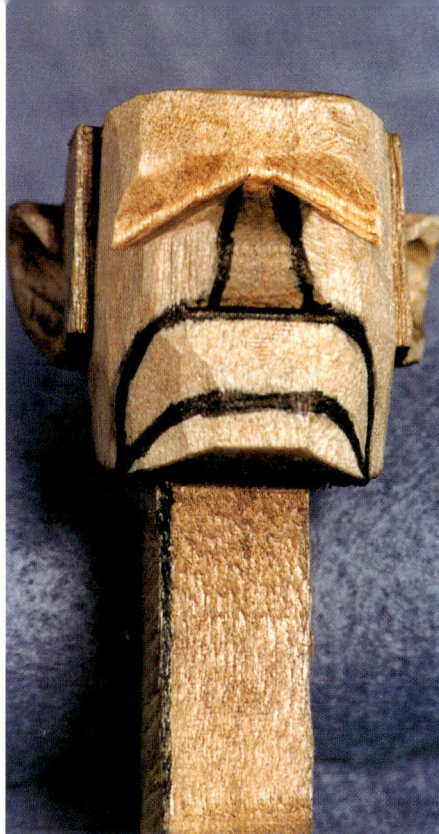

Using a **#39 1/4" "V" gouge**, cut in **horizontally** from the side of the face, toward the center, to create eye sockets.

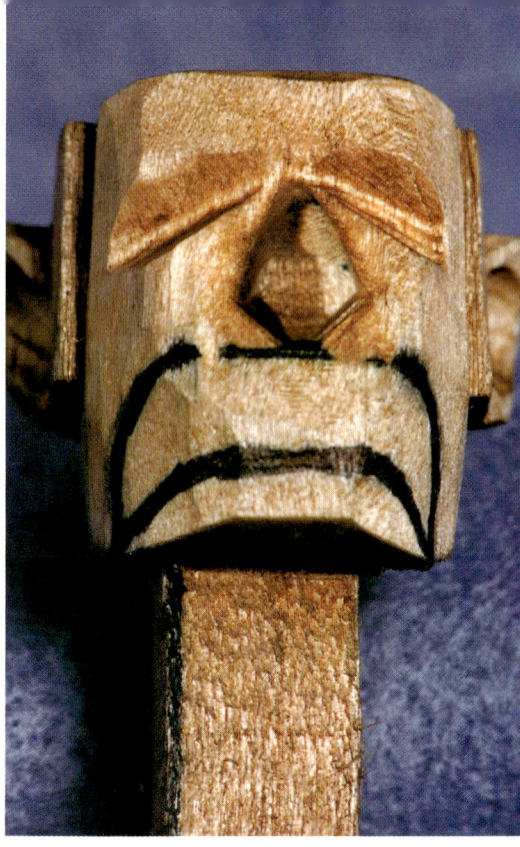

Remove the lower corners of the nose at about a 45 degree angle, using your knife.

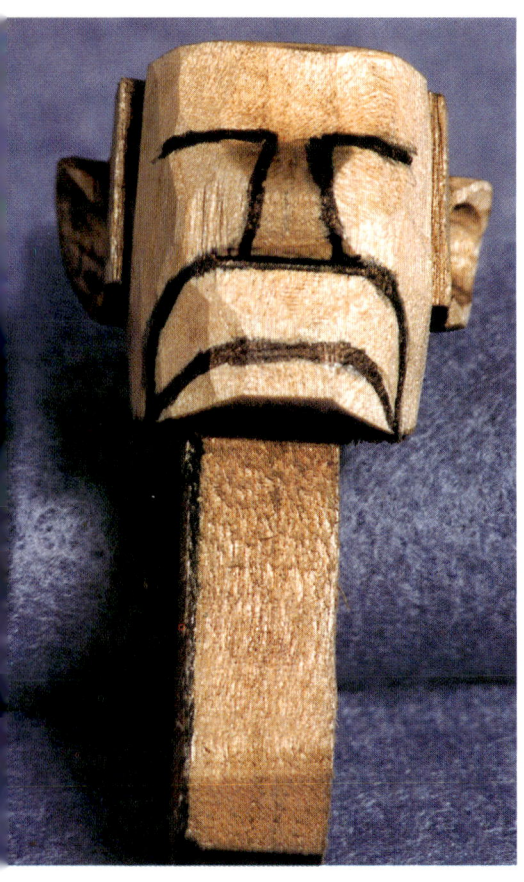

Sketch in the eye, nose and mustache lines.

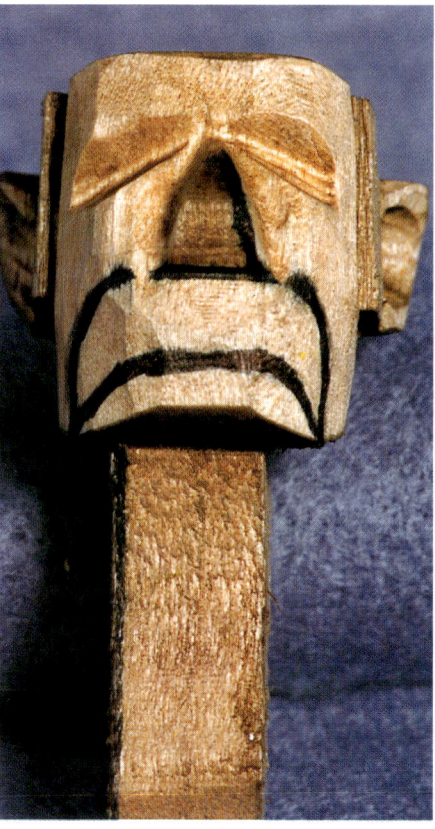

Again using the **#39 1/4" "V" gouge**, follow the nose lines, starting at the bottom of the nose and cutting up to the inside corner of the eye sockets.

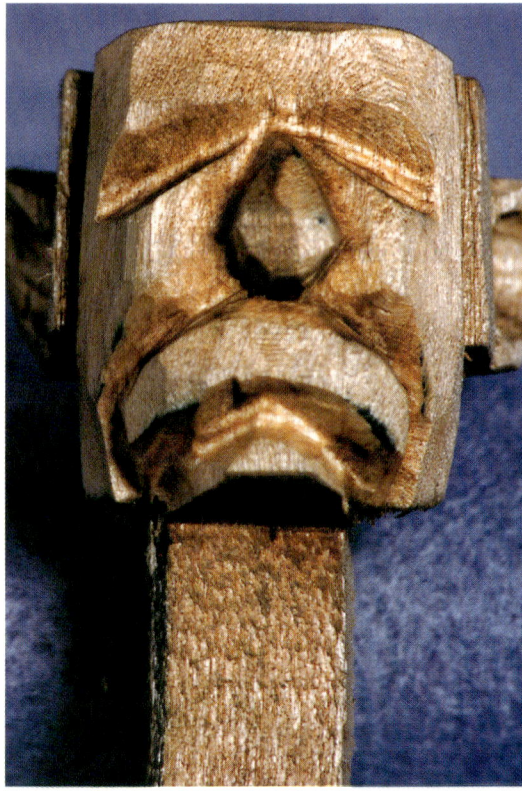

Now, use your **#39 1/4" "V" gouge** once more to follow the outlines of the mustache. (You will probably have to use your knife to remove wood from the portion of the mustache under the nose).

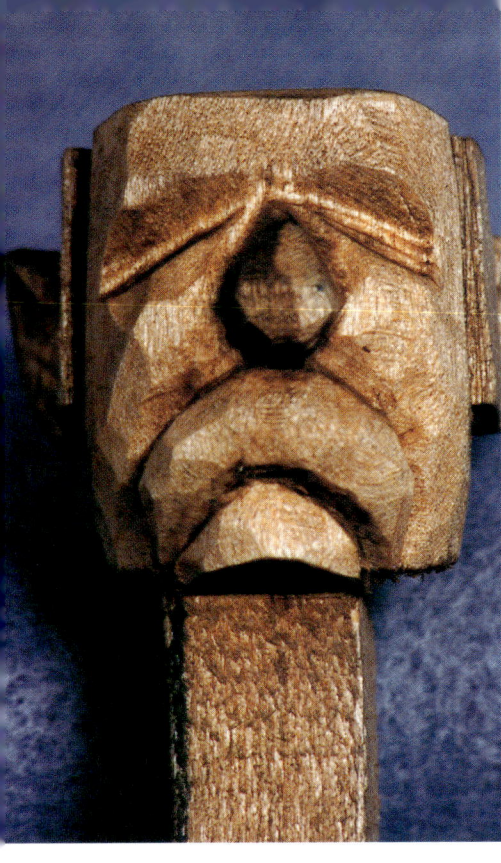

Use your knife to round off all the sharp edges of the nose, cheeks, lower eye sockets, and mustache.

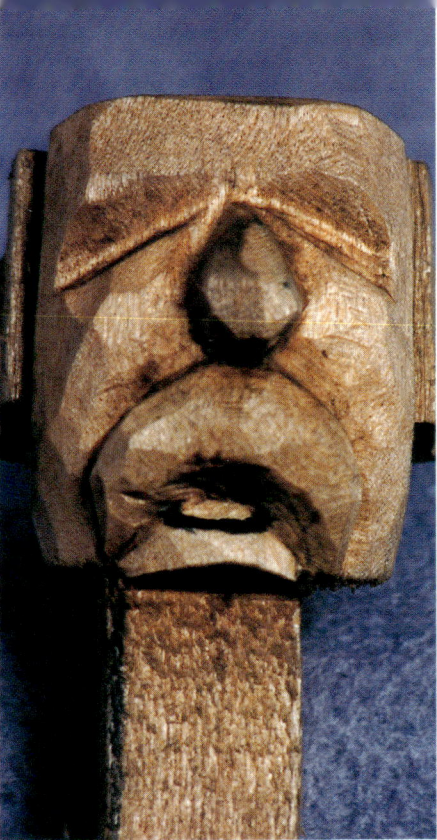

Draw a **horizontal** line to define the lower lip. Incise this line about 1/8" deep using the tip of your knife, then shave up toward it, so the lower lip stands out from the chin.

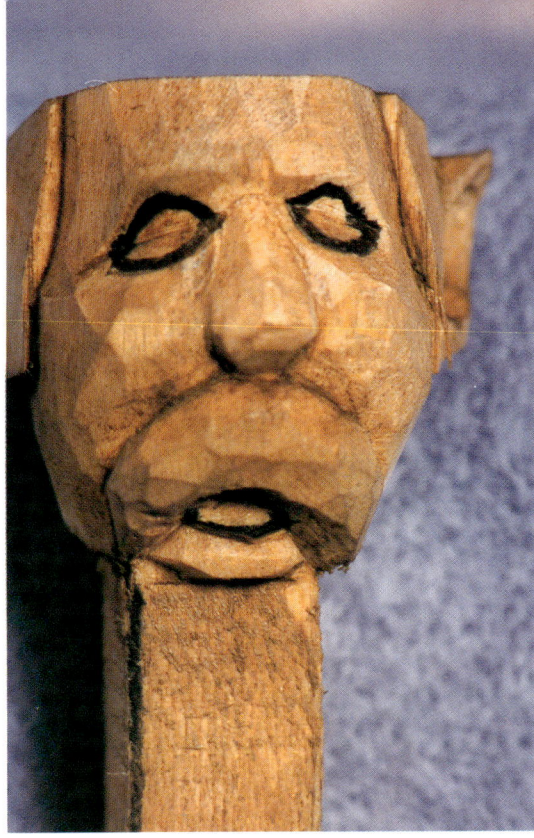

If you are going to use the quilt pin method for eyes, now is the time to do it. Refer back to the **TIPS** section for instructions. For this project, I will carve the eyes using the football method.

Sketch in the football shapes on the upper and lower halves of the eye sockets, and incise them with the tip of your knife. Refer back to the **TIPS** in the front of the book, to review this procedure.

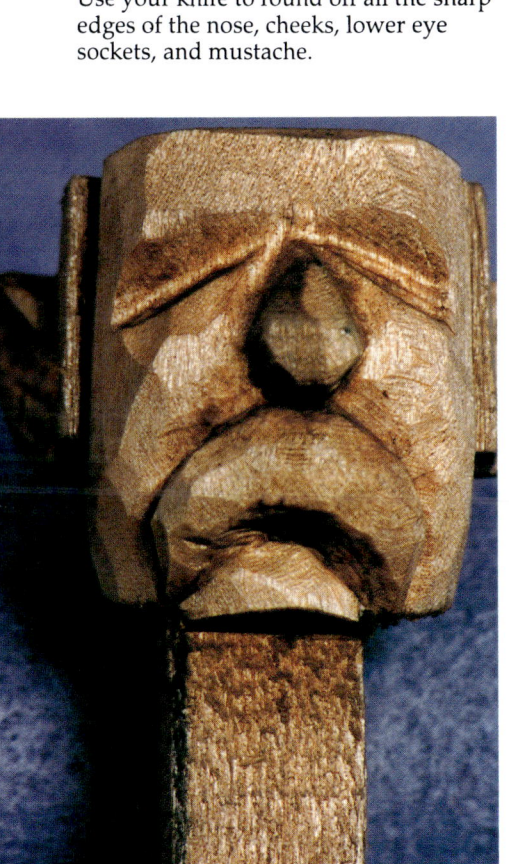

Remove a small portion of wood **below** the mustache, using a **#3 3mm flat gouge**. This will help define the chin, and will make the mustache more prominent.

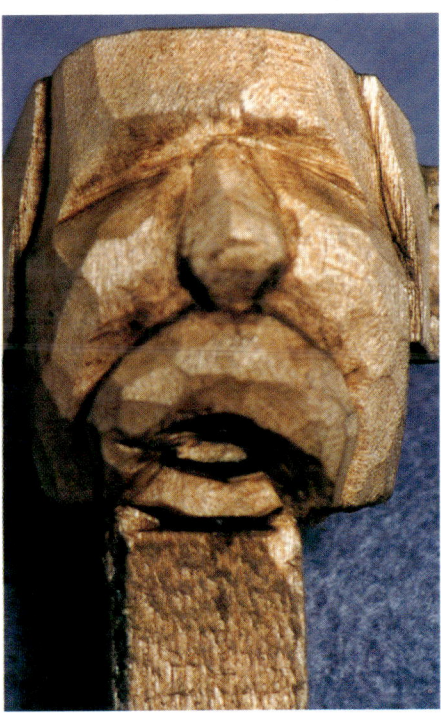

Starting at the lower outside edge of the eye socket, shave away a small amount of wood all the way to the top of the head, to define the cheek and temple area. Then, round off any sharp edges this step produced.

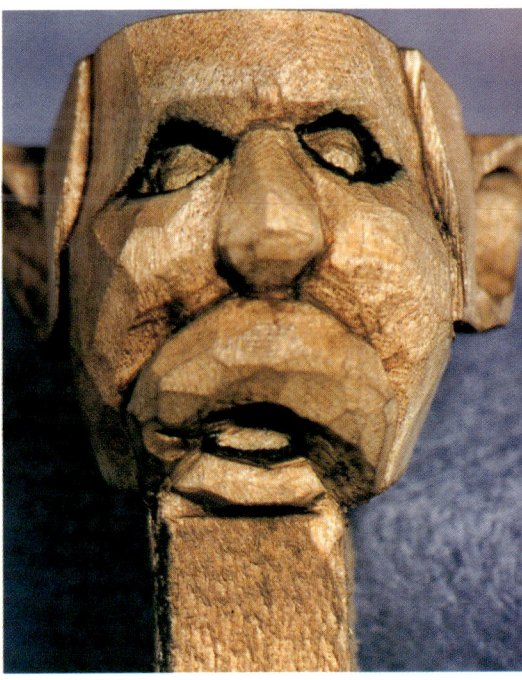

Use the tip of your knife to remove triangular shaped pieces of wood from the corners of the eyes.

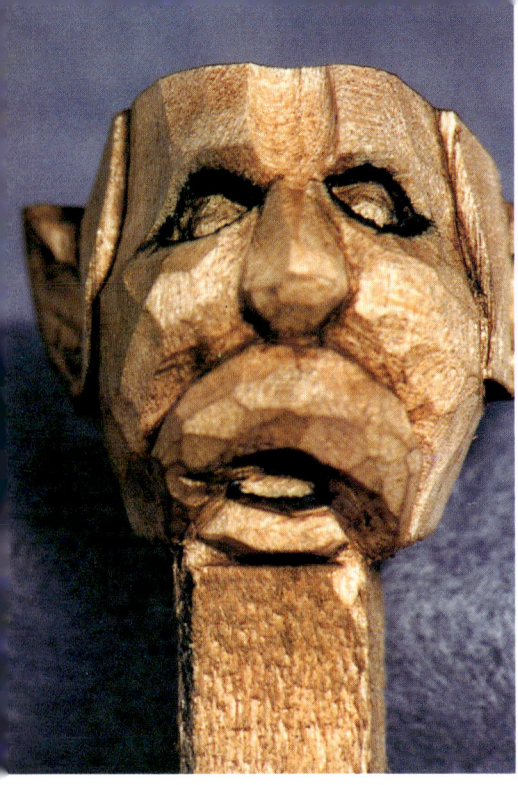

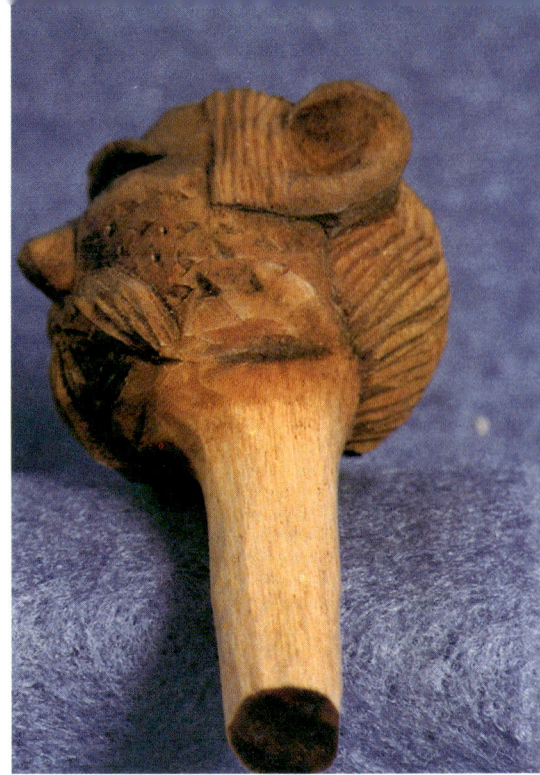

Remove a small amount of wood above the nose to form the ridge between the eyebrows using a **#7 3mm "U" gouge**.

Use a **#10 2mm "U"** or **#39 1/8" "V" gouge** to put detail into the hair and mustache. (Here is where having the hat removed is a big help!). If desired, add additional detail such as beard stubble now. Refer back to the TIPS section if this technique is new to you.

Now, remove the sharp corners from the **rear** edges of the neck. Go all around the neck, removing sharp edges, until you have a round neck. The size of the neck you end with will determine how big a hole you will drill in the body to receive it.

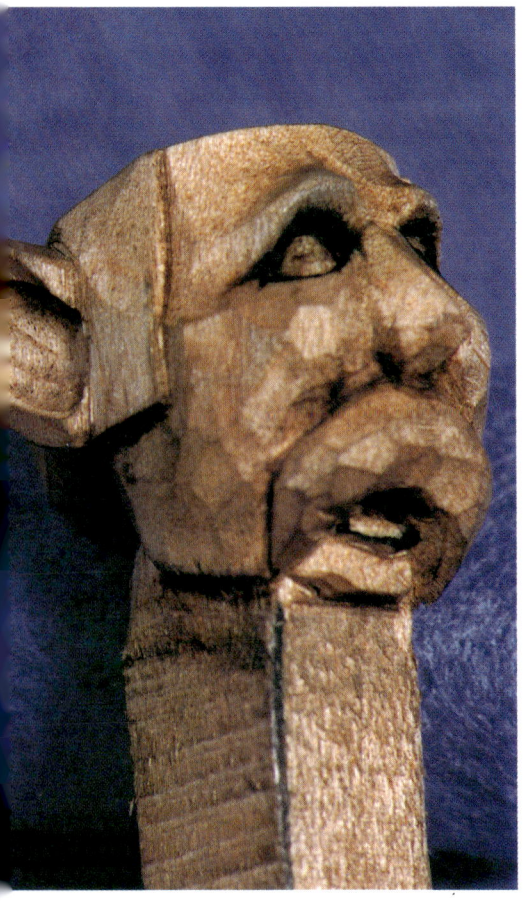

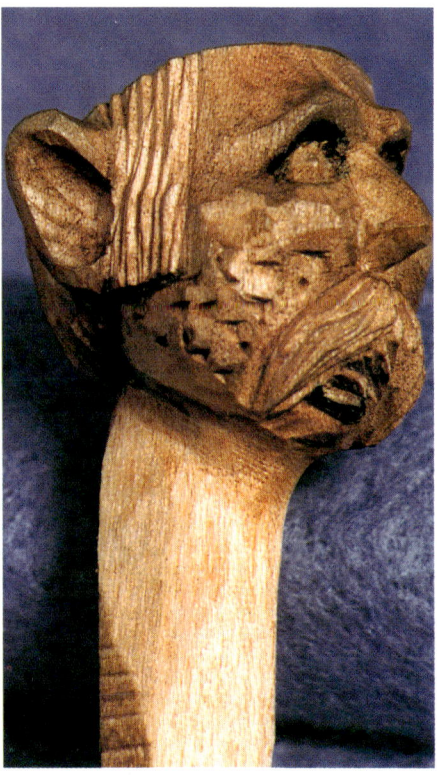

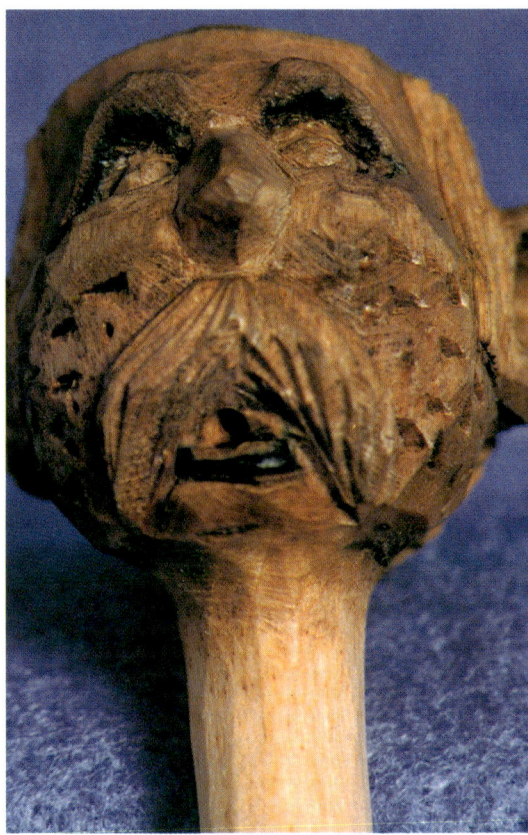

Take your knife tip, and with a curling motion, scoop away a small amount of wood slightly above each eye socket, on the forehead up to the top of the head, to form eyebrows.

Use your knife to remove the sharp edges from the chin and jaw, and from the two **front** edges of the neck. This will define the jaw line from the chin to the bottom of the ears, and will start the process of rounding the neck.

Use a small nail or drill bit to make a hole about 1/4" deep between the bottom of the mustache and the lower lip, for a cigarette.

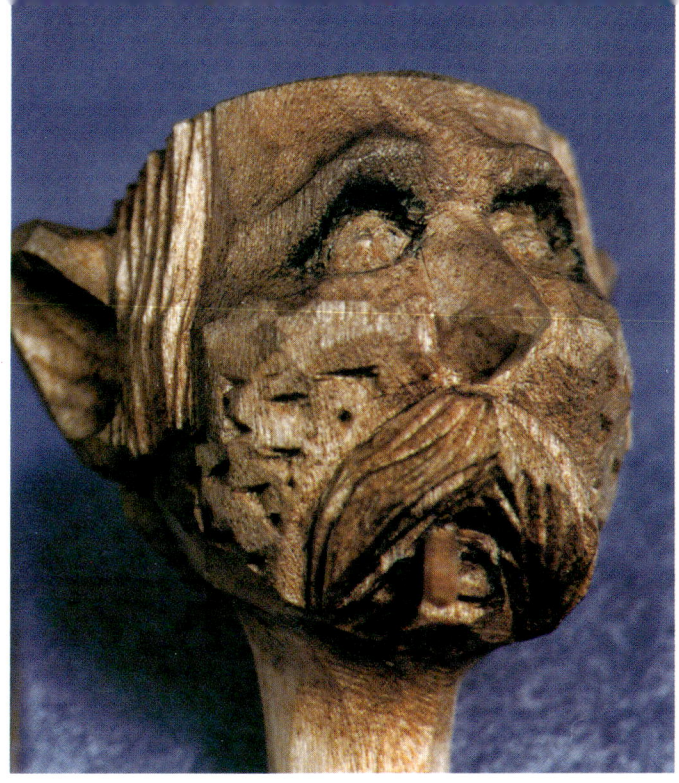

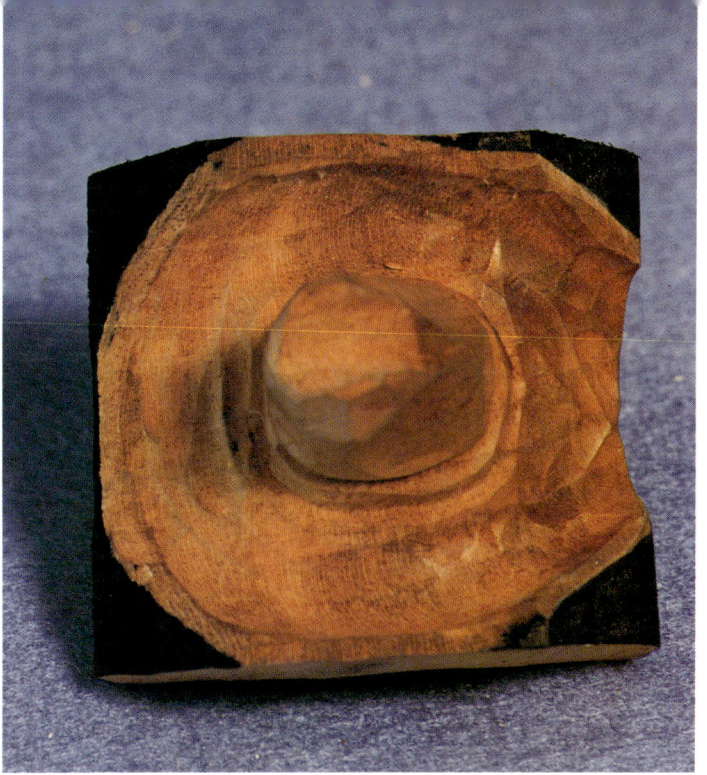

Trim a round toothpick so it will protrude about 1/4", after being inserted in the hole. When you are happy with the shape and length of your gunfighter's "smoke", put a small amount of glue on the end of the cigarette and insert it firmly into the hole.

To complete the rough shaping of the hat, use your knife to cut away the darkened sections of the brim, as shown in the photo.

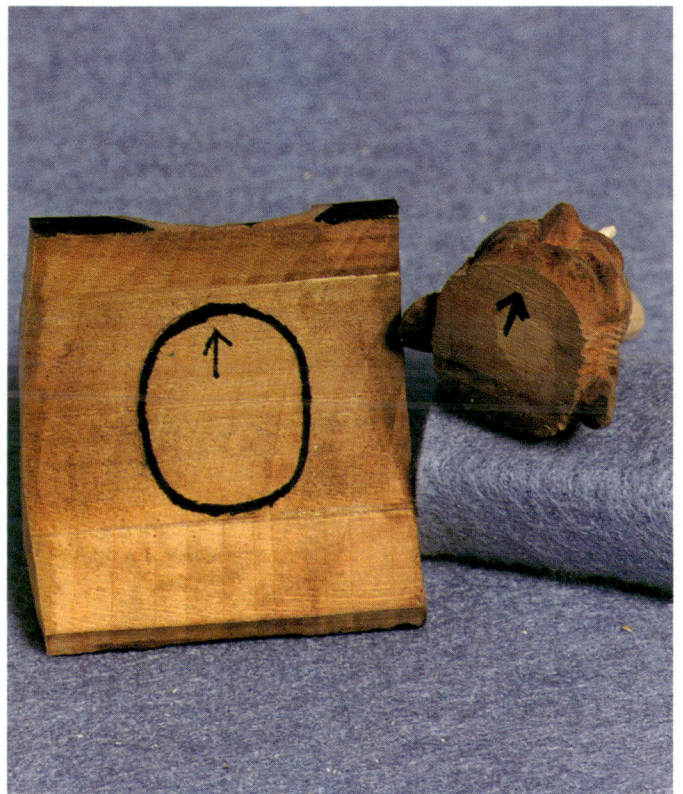

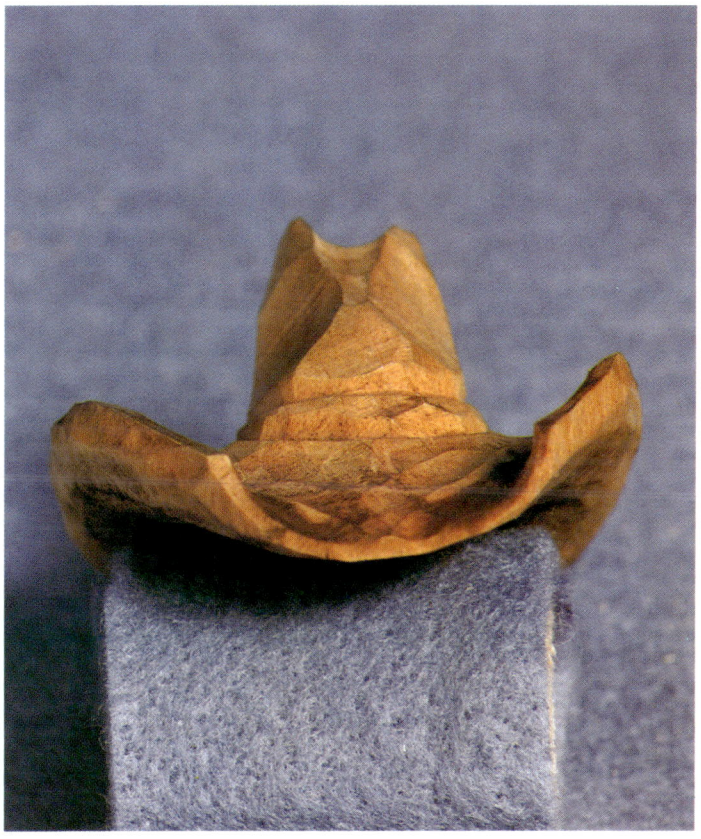

At this point, we are finished with the head and face carving. Look it over, and remove any sharp edges that don't appeal to you. When you are satisfied, hold the head against the bottom of the hat, centered under the crown. Trace around the head with a pencil to establish a reference line, then set the head aside temporarily so you can finish carving the hat.

Now, use your knife to **gently** remove the sharp edges from the underside of the hat brim. Be careful not to carve past the reference line. (You need to keep that area flat, so the head will glue flush to the hat).

This completes the head and hat carving. After we paint the head and hat, we'll glue them together. Now, we need to make a body for the head to sit on.

CARVING THE BODY

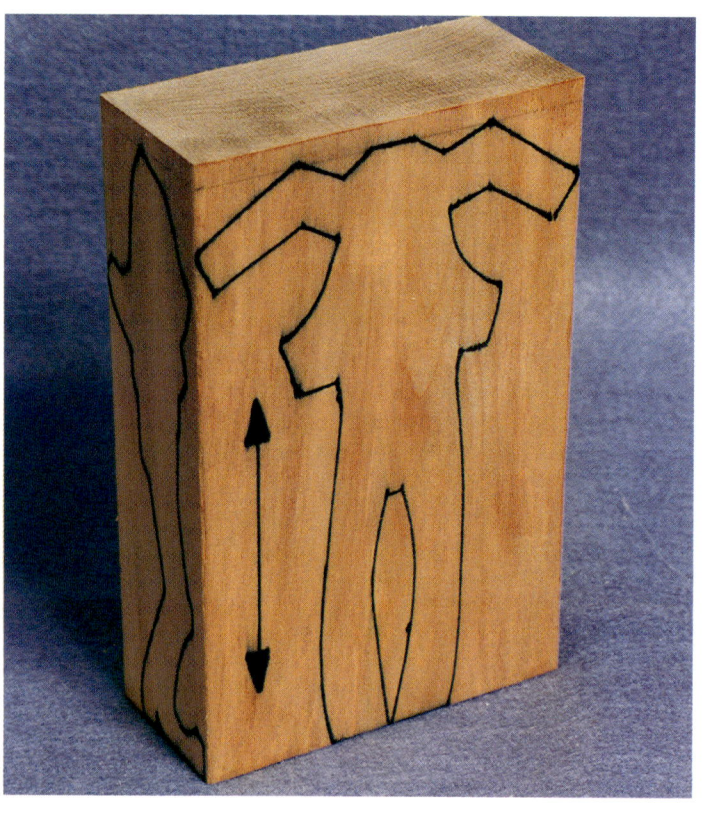

Transfer the side and front views of the body pattern to a block of wood. Note the grain direction runs **vertically** from the feet to the shoulders.

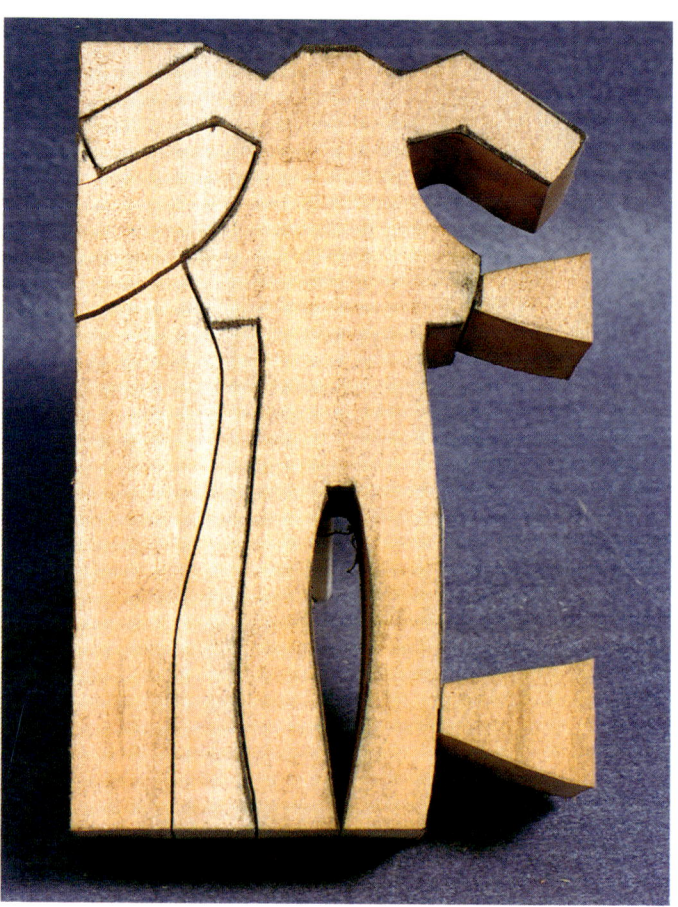

As you can see here, I have made a series of saw cuts on the **right** side of the body, but I haven't actually removed any of the wood. These will serve as references so I will know where to remove wood later, after I saw out the side profile.

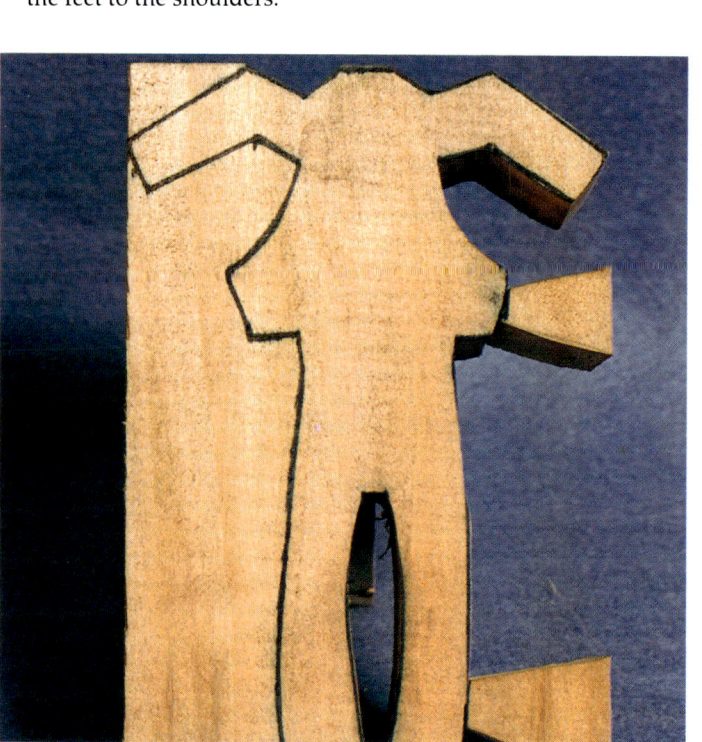

Using a bandsaw or other means, saw out the portion of wood between the legs. Then, saw out the **left** side of the body. Note the small tabs I left in place to help hold the body level when I saw out the side profile. We'll cut these off in a later step.

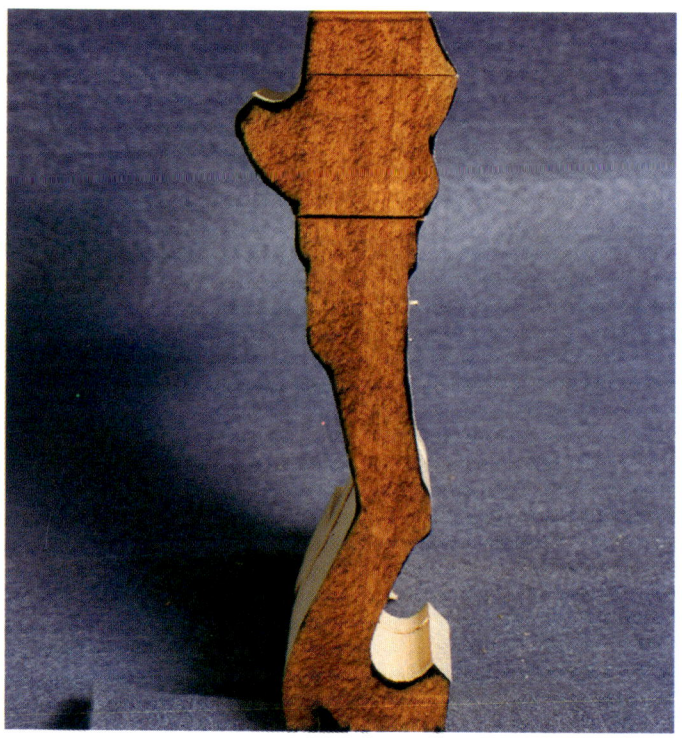

Turn the wood on its edge, and saw out the side view. Here is where the tabs are handy in helping keep the wood level.

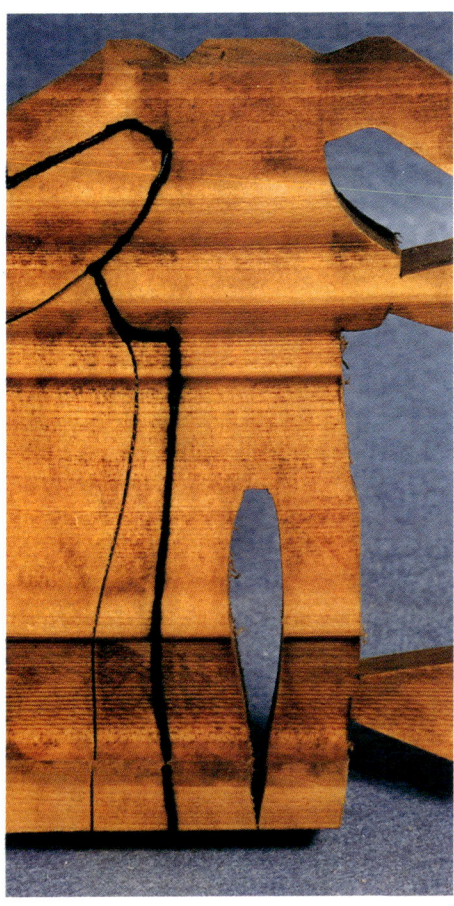

Now sketch in the right side of the front view, using the reference cuts you made earlier as a guide.

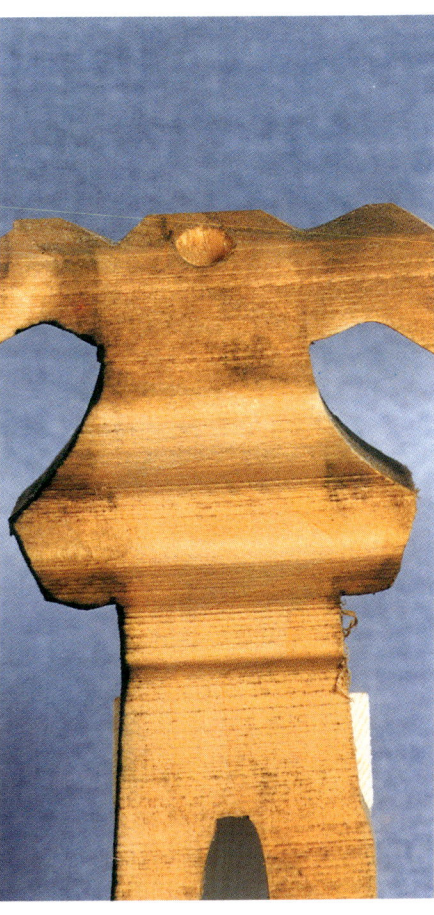

To make a hole in the collar for the neck, use a drill bit that is slightly larger than the neck you carved, and drill a hole straight down into the body, about 1/2" deep. You may want to clamp the body in a vise while you do this.

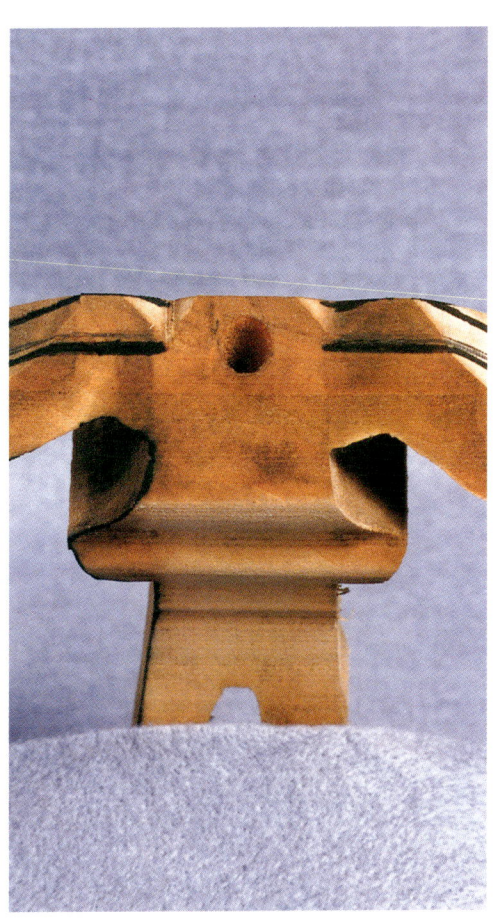

Sketch in the left and right arms across the top of the body.

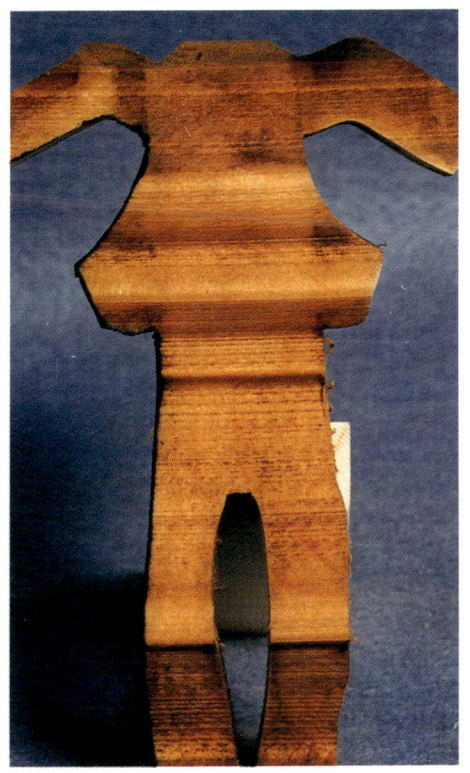

Finish sawing out the right side of the body, and also saw off the tabs at this time.

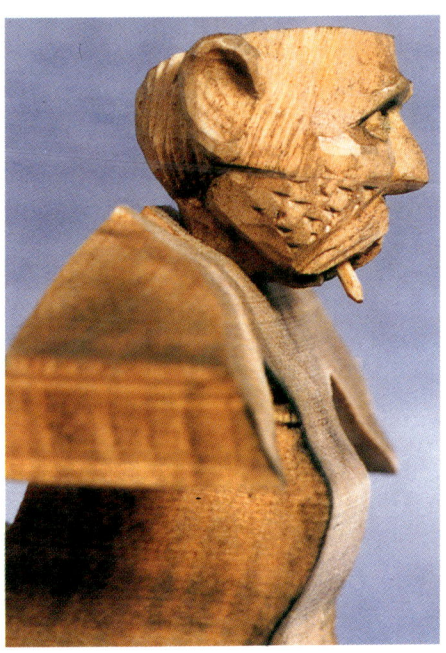

Trim and taper the neck as needed, to make a snug fit in the neck hole. Adjust the length so the head rests against the top of the body.

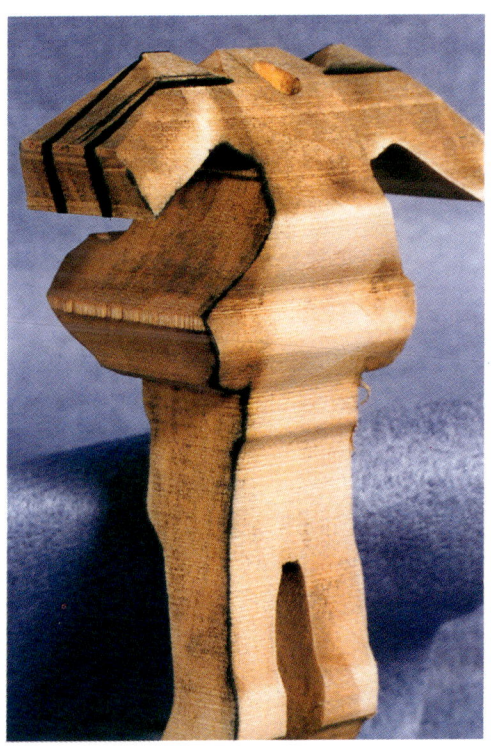

Carry these lines around and across the ends of the arms. You want the arms to be approximately as wide as they are thick, so they will be proportional when we round them off.

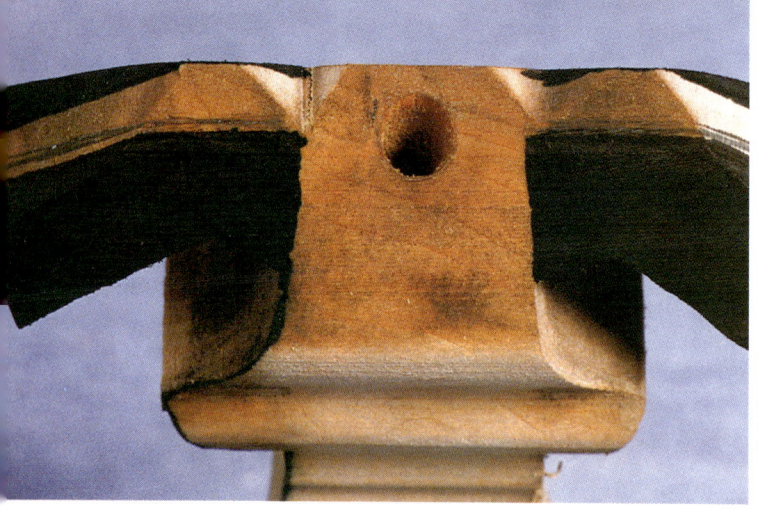

Use your knife or a **#3 10mm flat gouge** to remove the darkened sections of wood. Since the grain runs vertically, the wood will come off rather easily if you slice toward the body from the outside end of each arm. Use care not to break the arms off, but if you do just glue the arm back in place, and finish carving it when the glue dries.

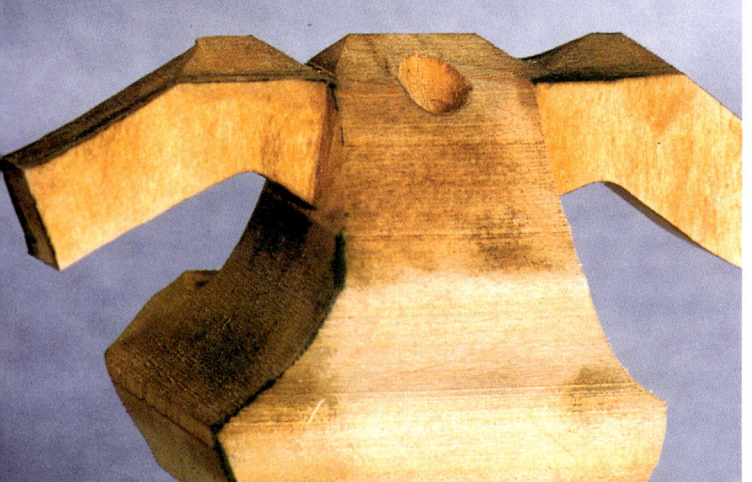

The arms and body so far.

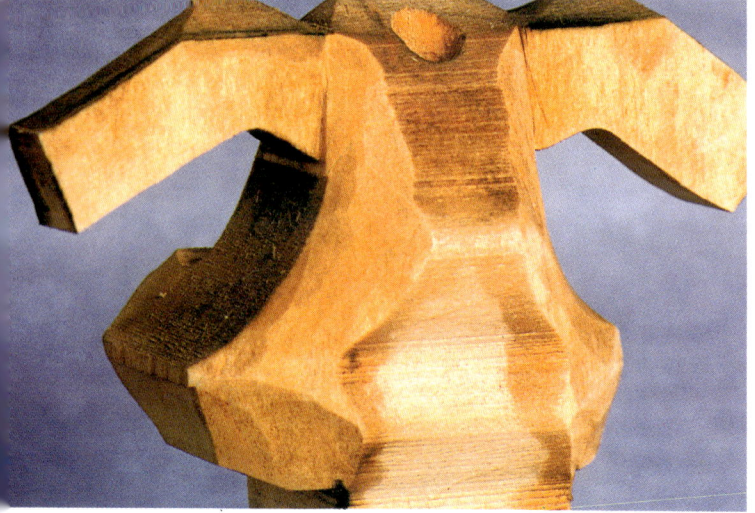

Knock off the two front corners of the coat with your knife. Then remove any sharp edges, until the coat blends smoothly into the arms in front.

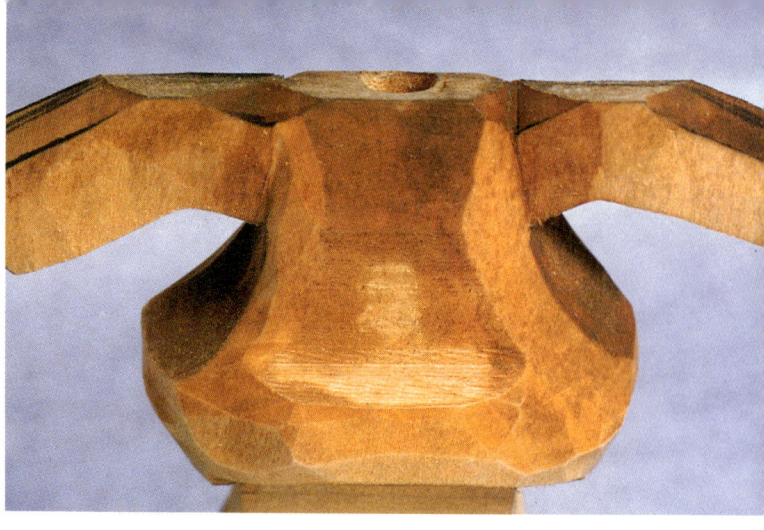

Now knock off the two rear corners of the coat, as you did in front. Remove any sharp edges so the coat blends smoothly into the arms in back.

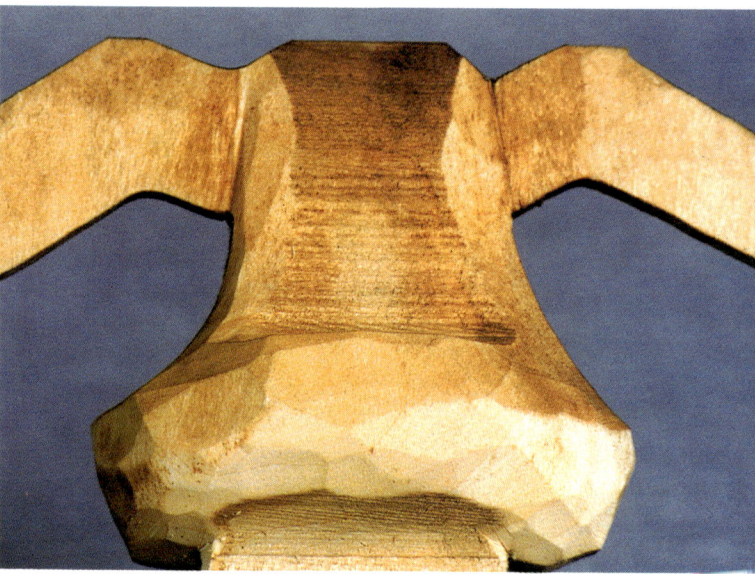

Next, round off the lower back edge of the coat, so it flows smoothly from the sides around to the center of the back.

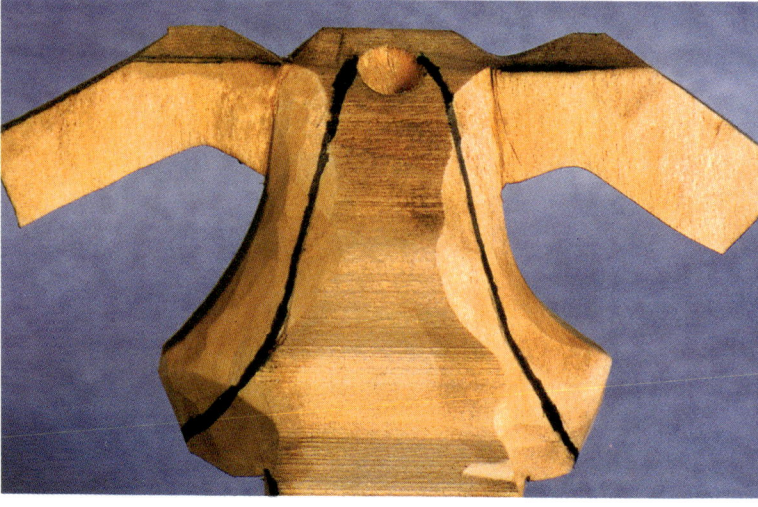

Draw left and right coat lines down the front of the body and around the sides.

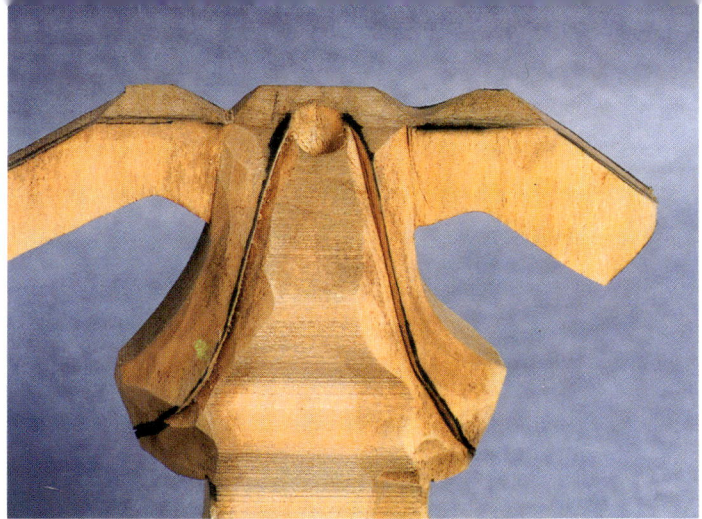

Incise the lines about 1/8" deep with your knife. Shave toward them from the center of the body to separate the coat from the bandanna and vest.

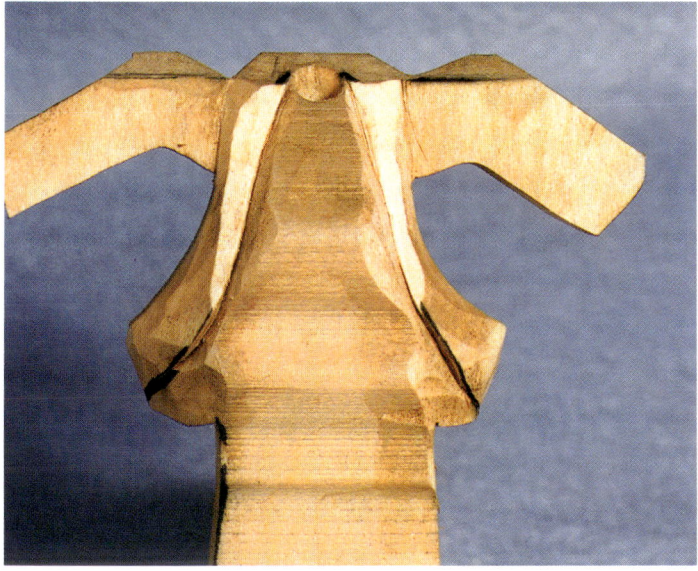

Trim down the front edges of the coat so the bandanna stands out, then remove any sharp edges you created.

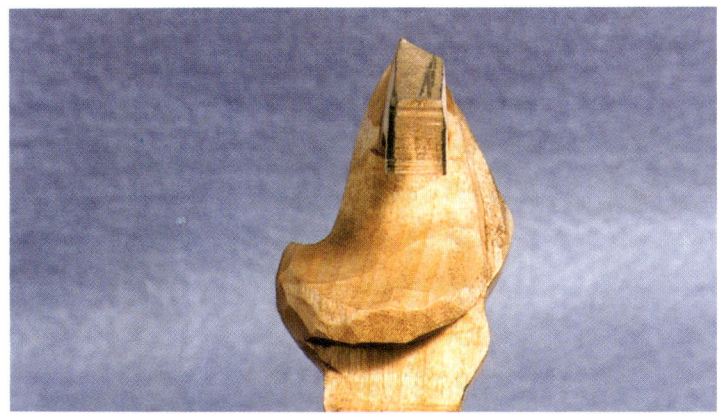

Remove wood on the sides, so the coat flows smoothly around from the front to the back. Also round off the side edges of the coat, and the area of the coat that is under the arms.

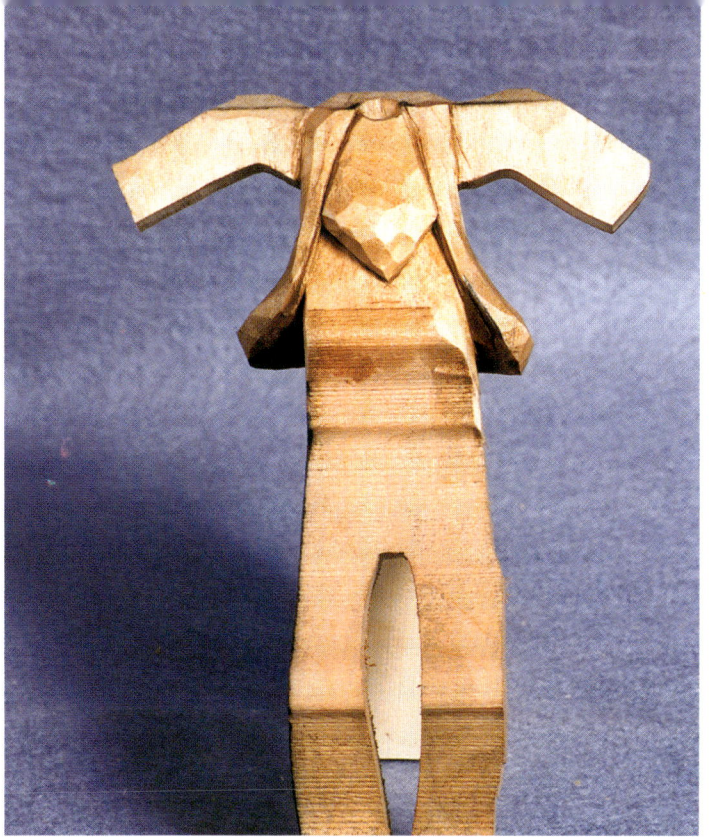

Draw lines to indicate the bottom of the bandanna. Incise the lines about 1/8" deep and shave up towards them. Round off all sharp edges on the lower end of the bandanna.

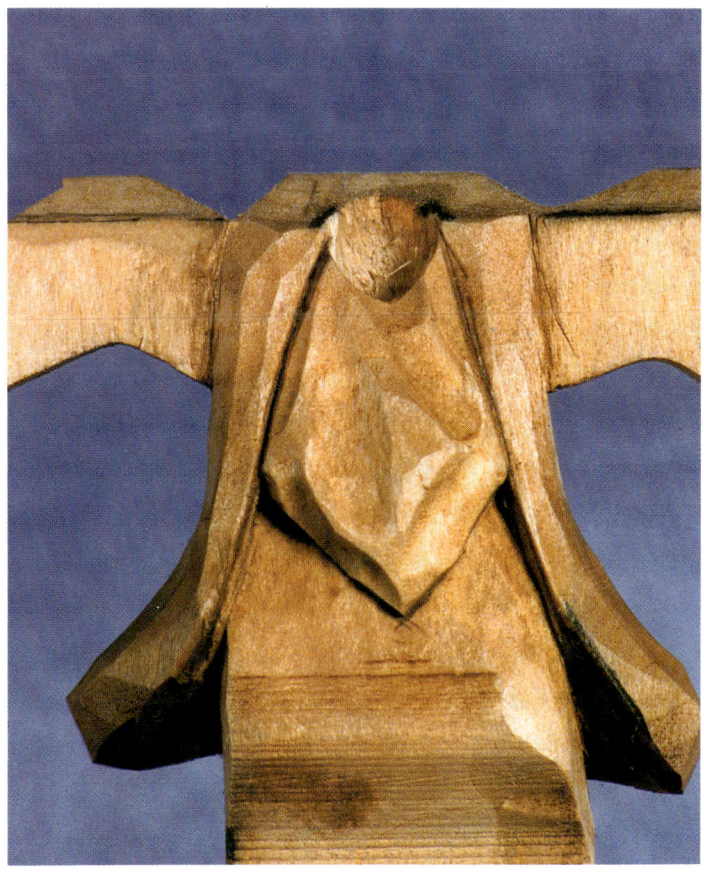

Use a **#10 6mm "U" gouge** to scoop out the neck area at the top of the bandanna, and also to cut some wrinkles and folds into the bandanna.

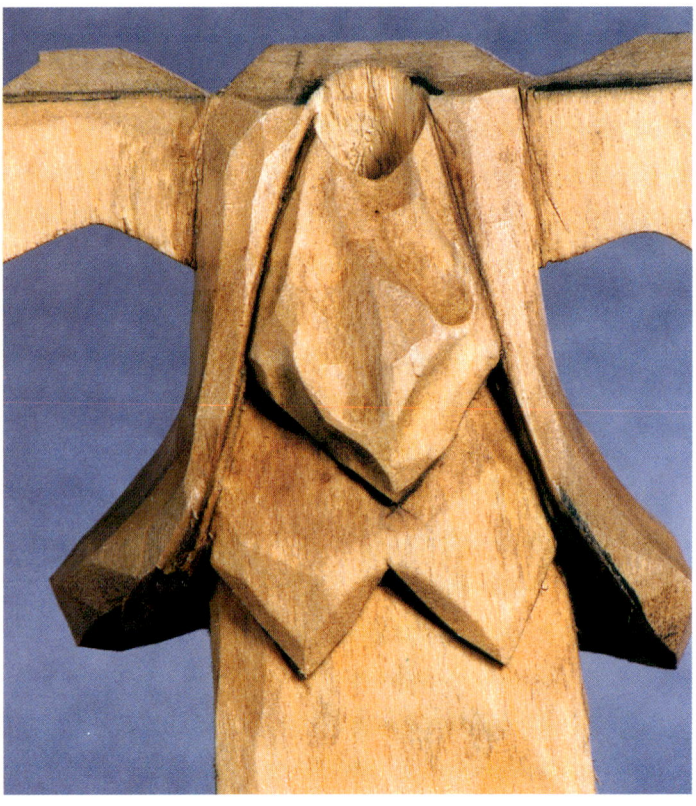

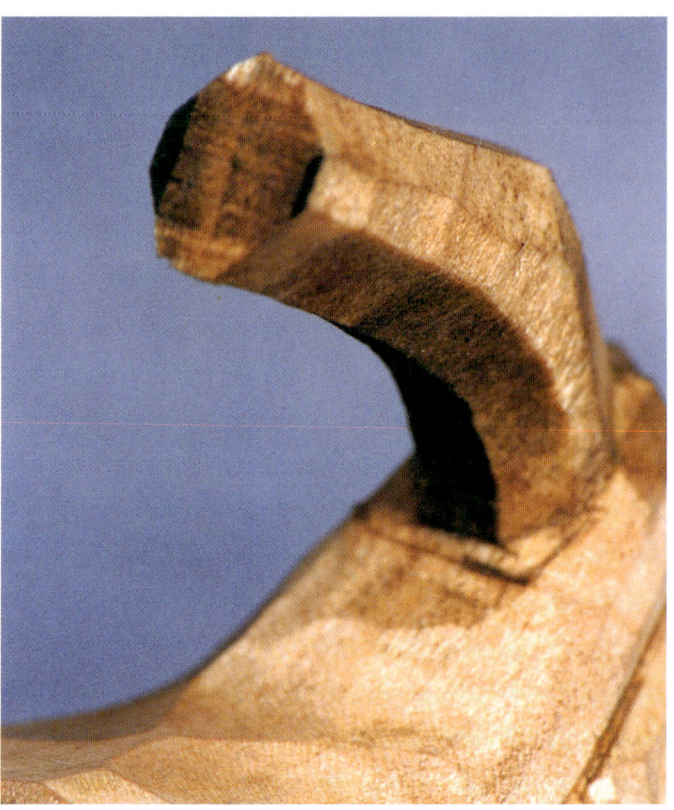

Draw the vest lines. Incise them about 1/8" deep and shave up toward them, so the vest will stand out from the shirt.

Now that we are about through swinging knives and gouges around the top of the body, let's reduce the size of the arms, finish the coat, and start on the shirt and lower part of the body. First, use your knife to remove the four sharp edges on each arm and bring them to an octagonal shape.

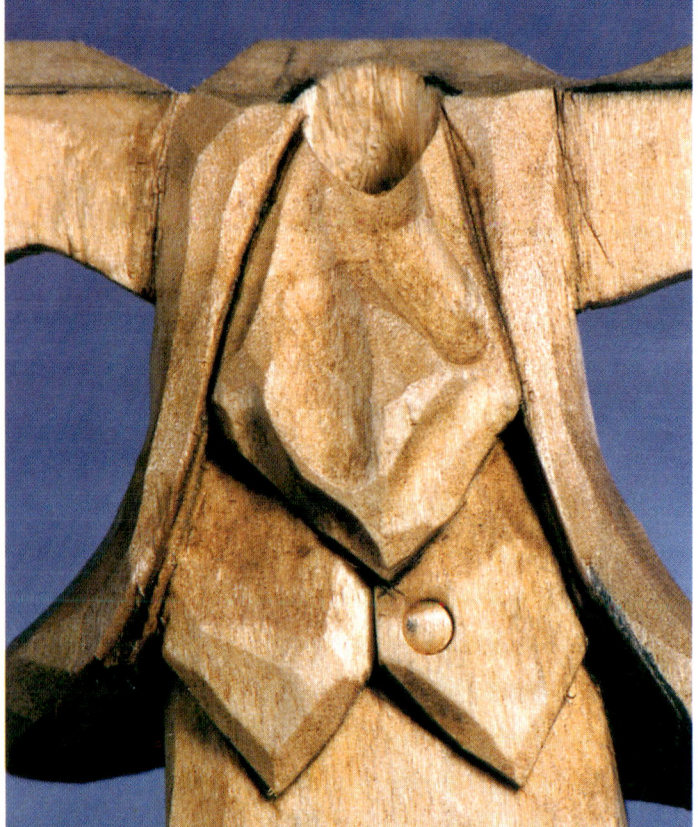

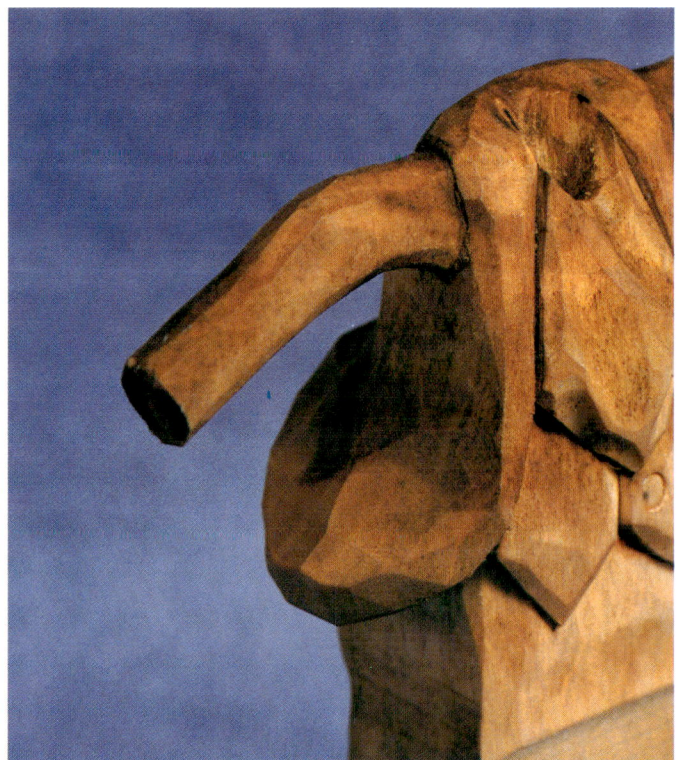

Incise a shallow vertical line up the approximate center of the vest. Shave toward it from the right side of the vest, so the left side will appear to be slightly higher. Use an eye punch or nailset to add one or two buttons as desired.

Remove the new sharp edges you just created, and the arms should now be round enough to live with. (Experienced carvers may want to add extra folds and wrinkles, as desired).

46

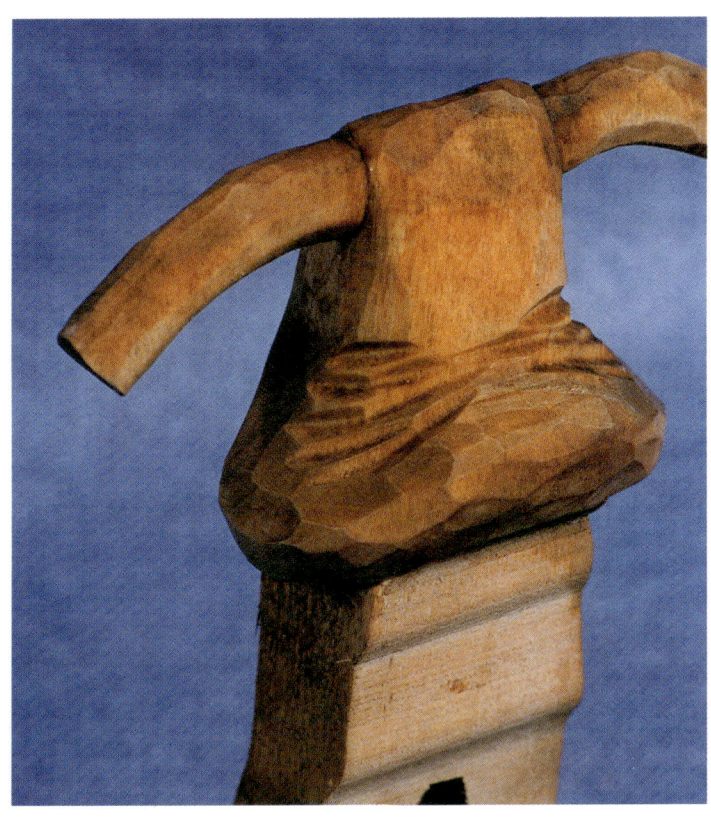

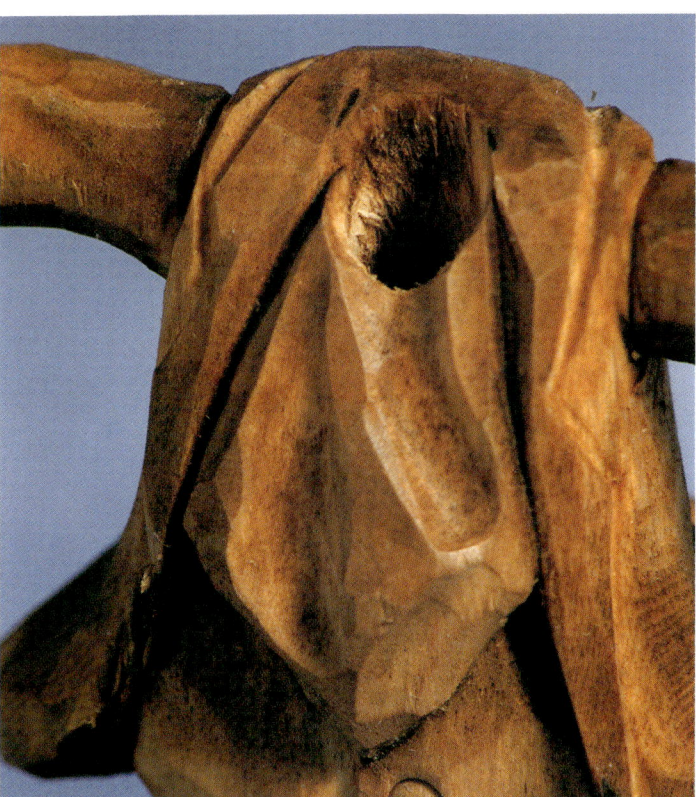

Round off any sharp edges still remaining on the back of the coat, then use a **#39 1/4" "V" gouge** to cut some wrinkles in the curl of the coat on the left and right sides.

Sketch in the lapels on the front of the coat, and carry the line around the back of the neck to form the collar. Follow along these lines with the **#39 1/8" "V" gouge** to define the lapels and collar.

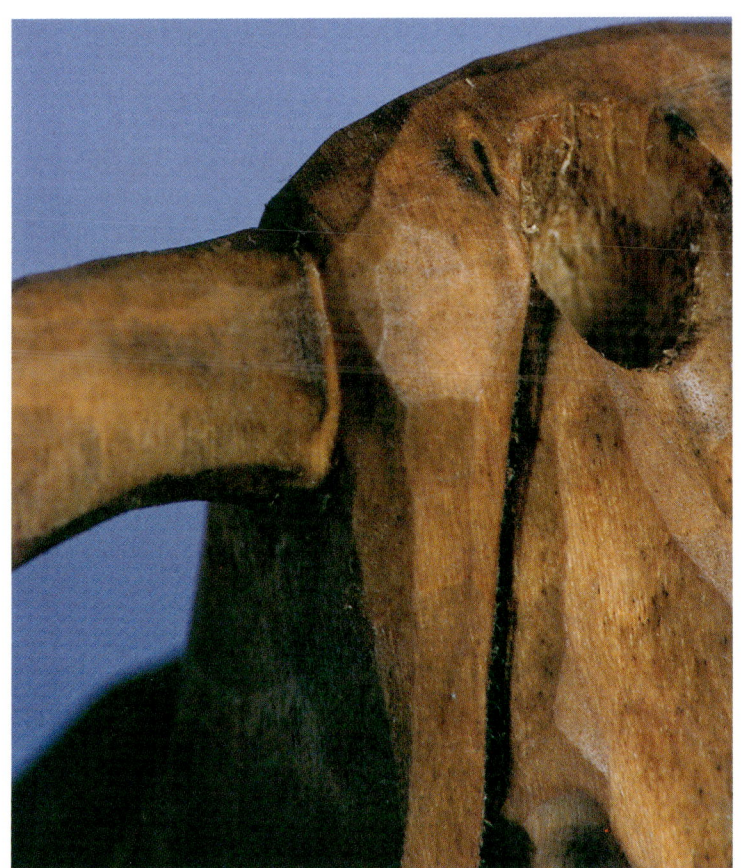

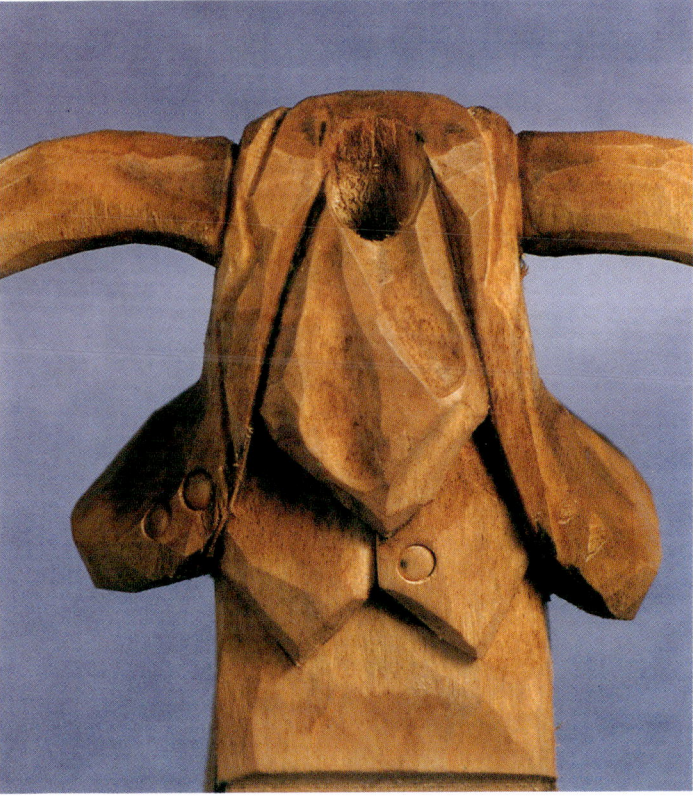

A **#39 1/8" "V" gouge** is used to cut a light seam around the sleeves, where they join the coat.

Use an eye punch or nailset to add two buttons to the right side of the coat. Use the **#39 1/8" "V" gouge** to make two button holes on the left side of the coat.

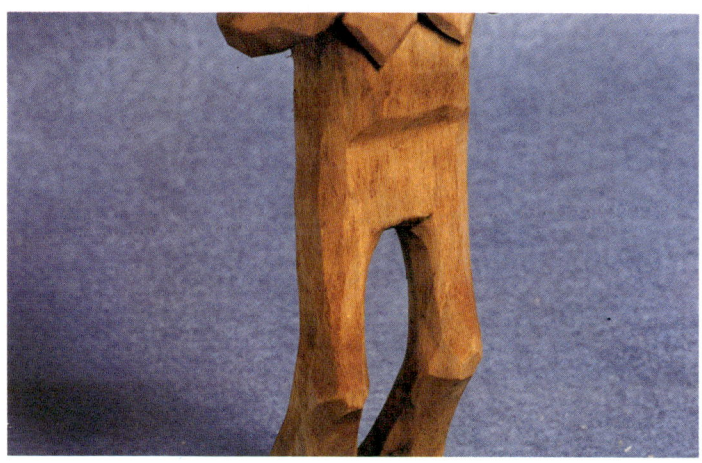

Use your knife to knock off all the sharp edges on the lower part of the body, **except** for the boots. We'll work on the boots last.

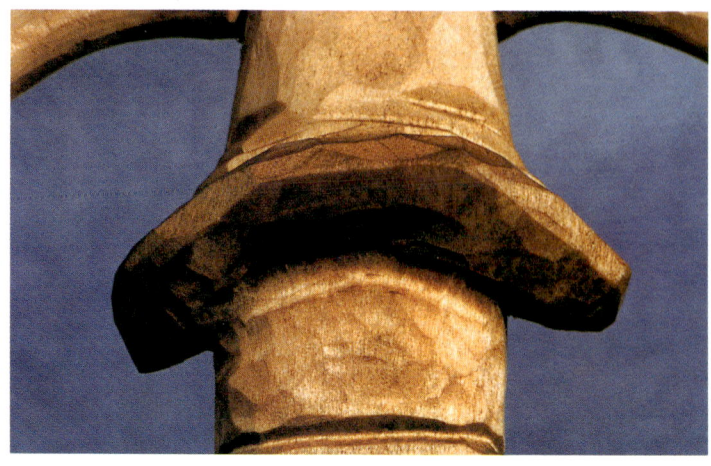

Here, I have removed some of the wood under the coat using a **#4 6mm small curved gouge**, to thin the coat and make it appear more realistic.

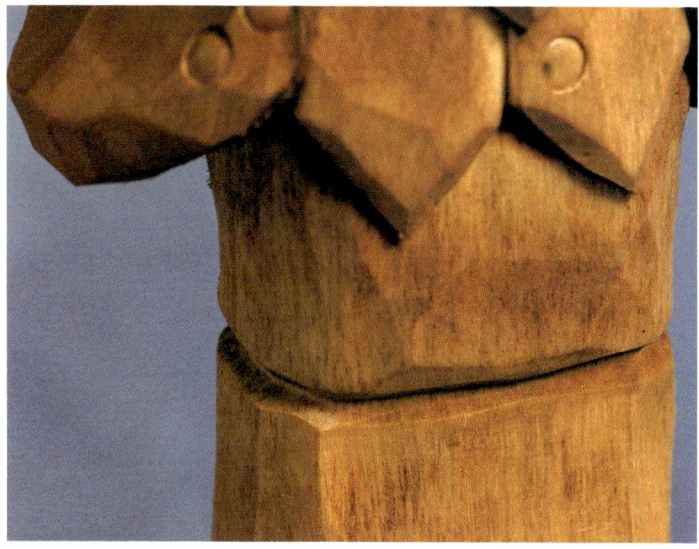

Draw a line around the body to define the shirt and pants separation. Follow this line using a **#39 1/4" "V" gouge** to further define the shirt and pants separation.

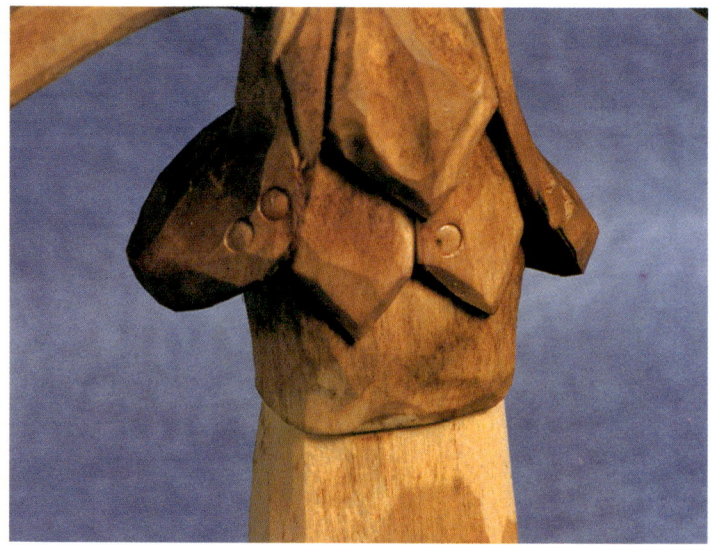

Now, go all around the body again, shaving from the legs up toward the shirt bottom, so the pants blend smoothly into the bottom of the shirt.

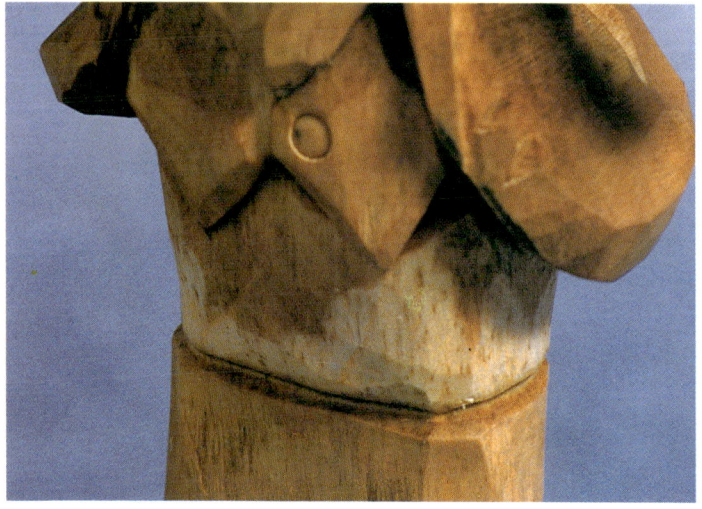

Use your knife and go completely around the body, rounding off all the sharp corners of the shirt.

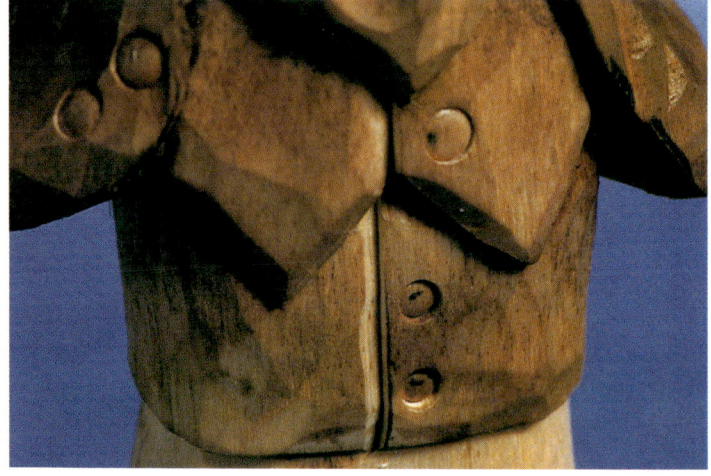

Incise a shallow vertical line up the approximate center of the shirt. Shave toward it from the right side of the shirt, so the left side will appear to be slightly higher. Use an eye punch or nailset to add one or two buttons as desired.

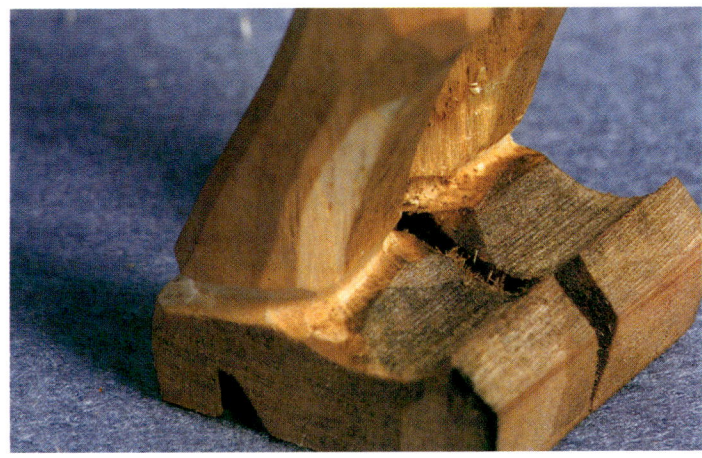

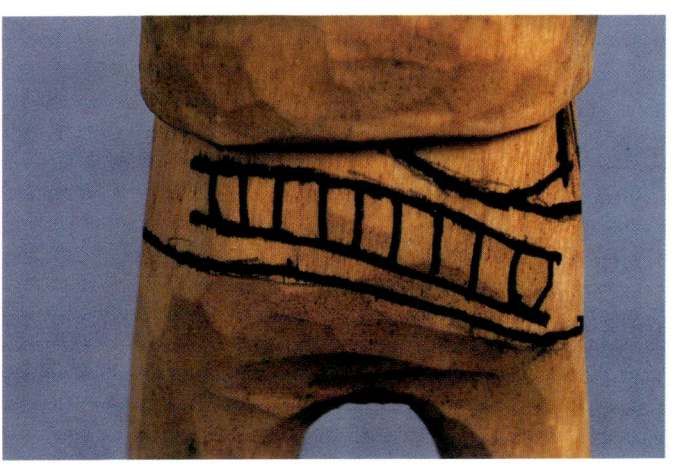

Sketch a line around the bottom of each leg, to define the hem of the pants. Follow this line with a **#39 1/4" "V" gouge** to separate the pants from the boots.

Continue the lines around the right side, left side, and across the back. On the back of the gunbelt you can see where I have also sketched in a cartridge loop section.

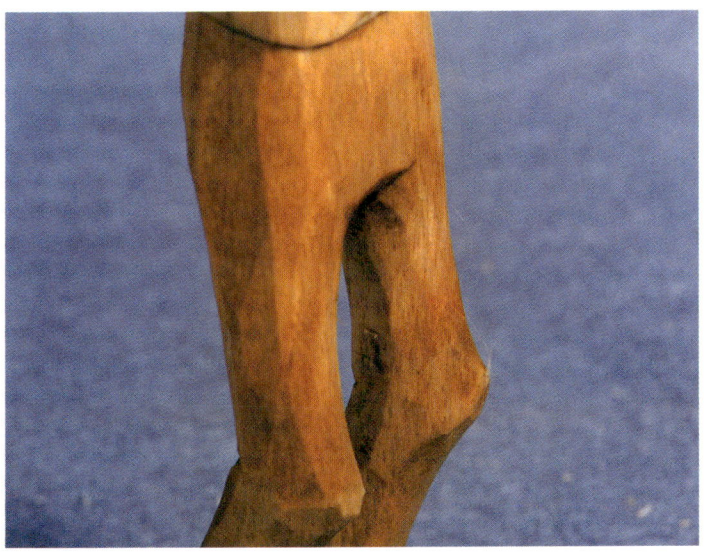

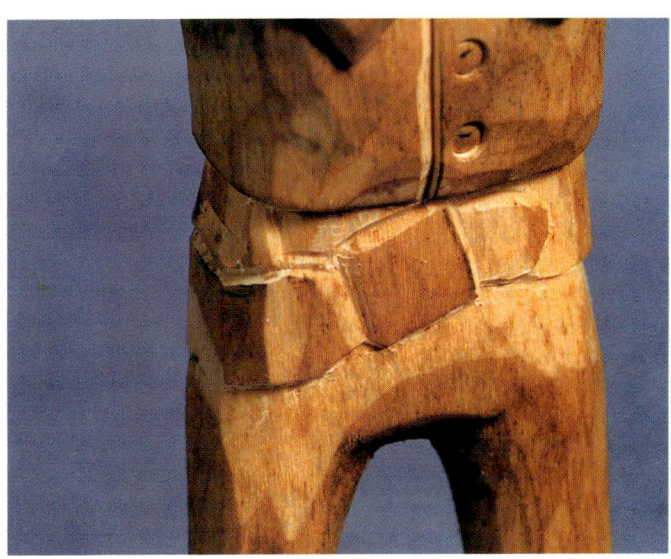

Use your knife to finish rounding and shaping the waist and legs, much the same way as you rounded the arms. **Leave a small, flat area on the side of the right leg, as we are going to attach a pistol there later.** Experienced carvers may add wrinkles and folds to the legs as they desire.

Now incise all the lines **except** the cartridge loop area about 1/16" deep, and shave **toward** them as appropriate, so you get details in front...

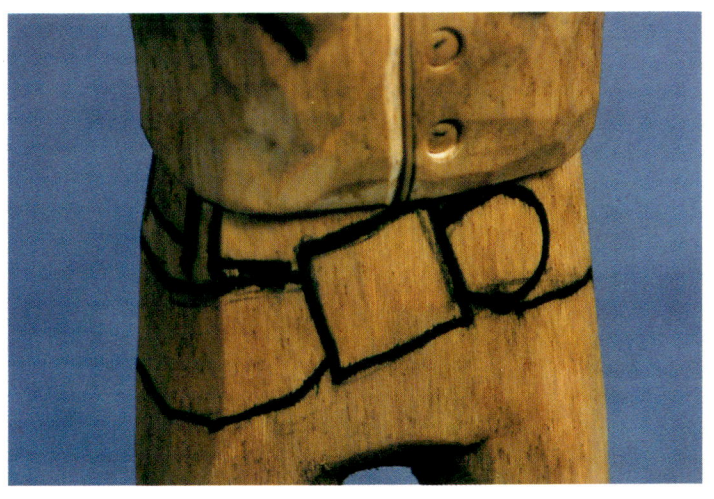

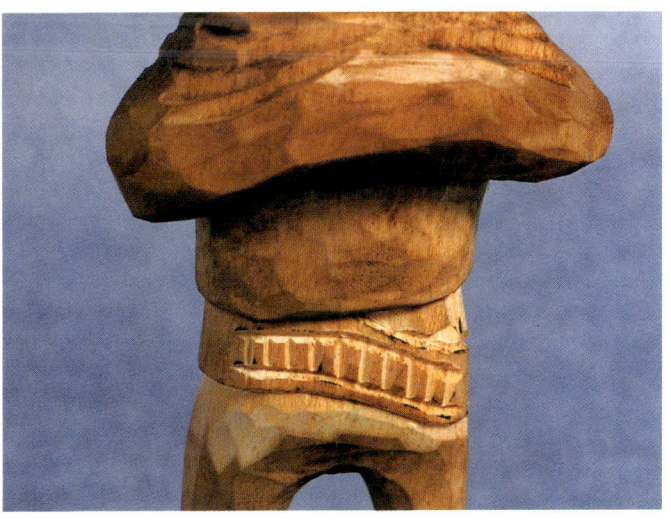

Sketch in the belt, belt loops, and gunbelt in front.

and in back. I detailed the cartridge loop area using a **#39 1/8" "V" gouge**, as it seems to work better in this area.

49

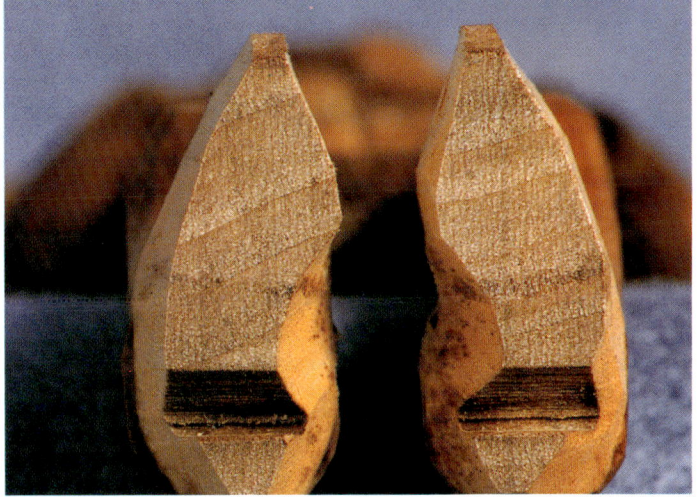

Use your knife to block out and shape the boots, as seen in this bottom view. You may be as serious or as comical as you want to be in shaping the boots. The choice is yours.

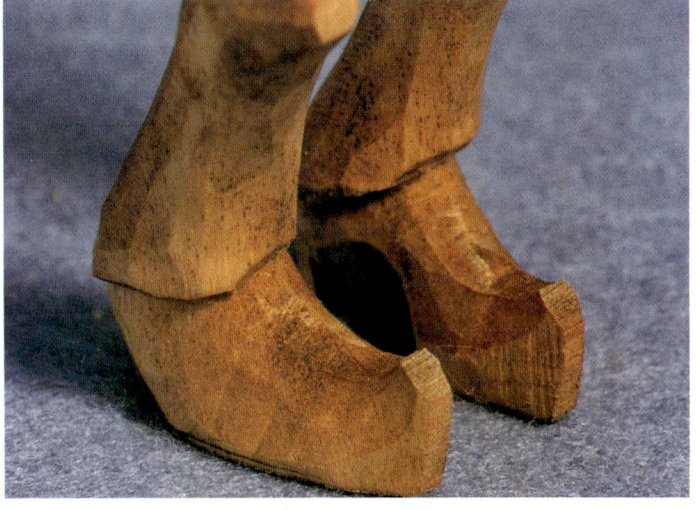

Round off all the sharp edges on the top side of the boots, and blend them smoothly into the bottom of the pants.

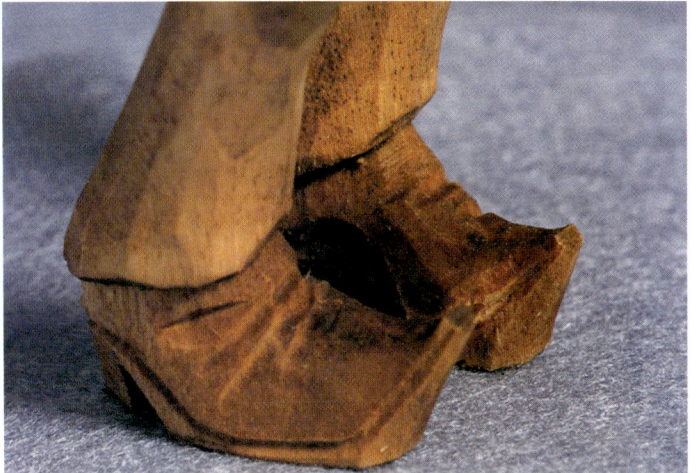

Shave the front corners of the toes down and back, so the toes will have a turned up appearance. This is another area you can do mildly, or can exaggerate for a more comical effect. Experienced carvers may want to add some cuts and wrinkles to the boots to "age" them a bit, and may want to use a **#39 1/8" "V" gouge** to add a sole line around the bottom edge of the boots.

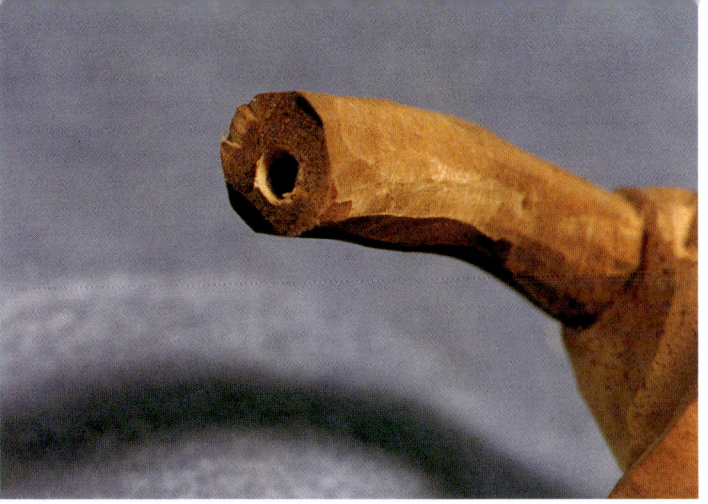

The last thing to do on the body is to drill some 1/8" holes about 1/4" deep into the ends of the arms. These holes will form sockets to insert the hands in at a later step.

This completes the body carving. Let's move on so we can get some hands and a pistol carved. You're doing just fine, so far. Stay with me, and soon we'll have a complete gunfighter!

CARVING THE HANDS

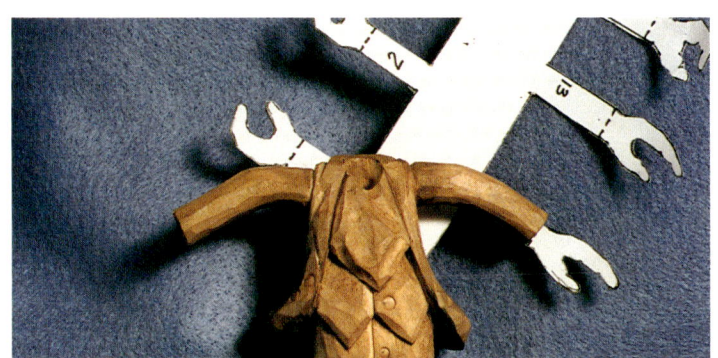

Now we'll get to put the hand template to work. The project pattern indicates that Hand #14 is the choice I used on the carving, for both hands.

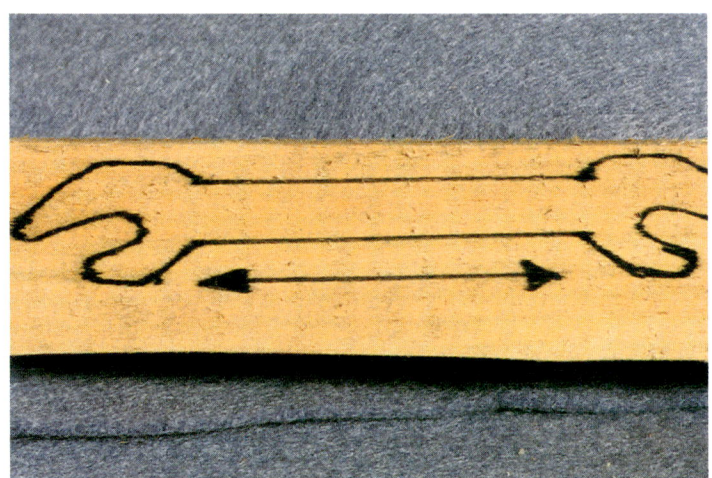

Lay out the top view of the hands on a piece of 3/4" thick basswood. Notice I have drawn both hands connected together by a short section of wood. This section will serve as a handle while I carve and shape the hands, and will form the wrist pegs in a later step. Saw out the top profile of the hands.

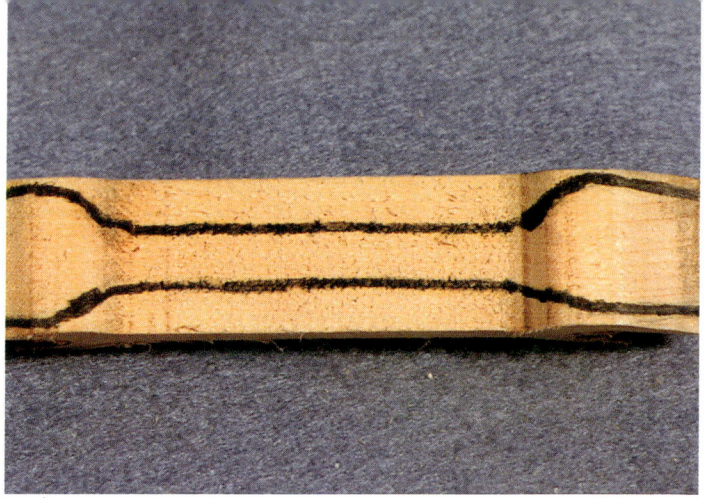

Now, using the top set of hands in the Hand Studies as a reference, sketch in the side profile of the hands, then saw them out. You now should have two hands that will require very little work to finish.

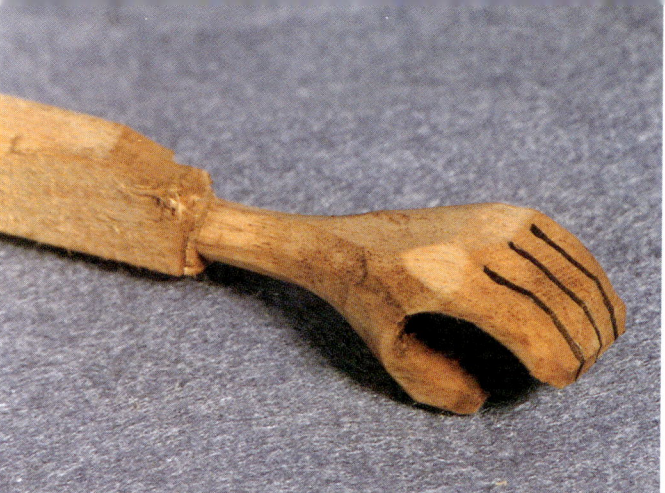

Draw a line in the middle of the finger section to divide it in half. Now draw lines to divide each of these sections in half. You should now have four fingers defined, all approximately equal.

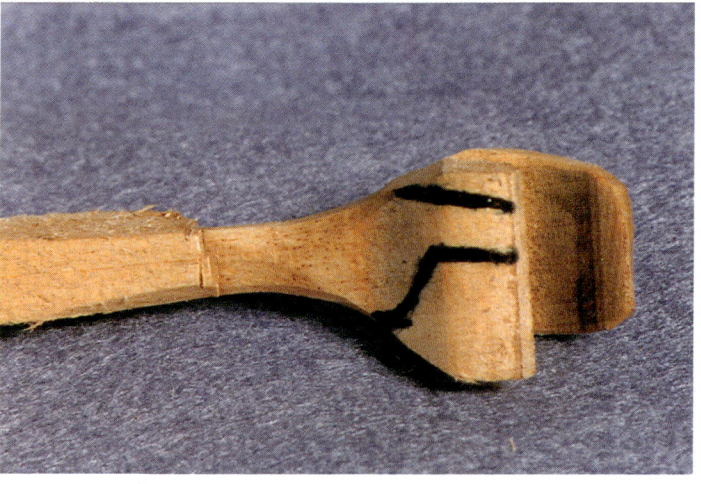

Use your knife and round off all the sharp edges of the hands. Next, sketch in the thumbs.

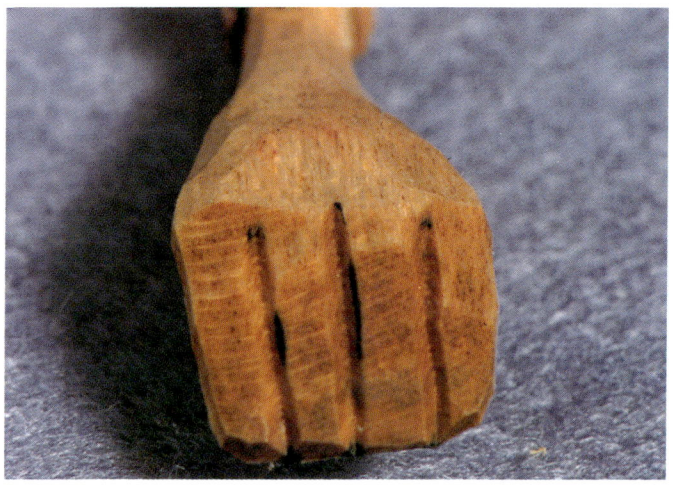

Using a **3mm #41 "V" gouge**, go over these lines so the fingers will be separated. *As an option,* to add further detail without too much pain on your part, use a bandsaw, scroll saw or coping saw to carefully saw along these lines. Use your knife to remove any fuzzy wood caused by the saw cuts. At this point, if you do nothing else, you will have two hands that will look perfectly good once they are painted. Experienced carvers may add more detailing as they desire, such as knuckles and wrinkles on the finger joints.

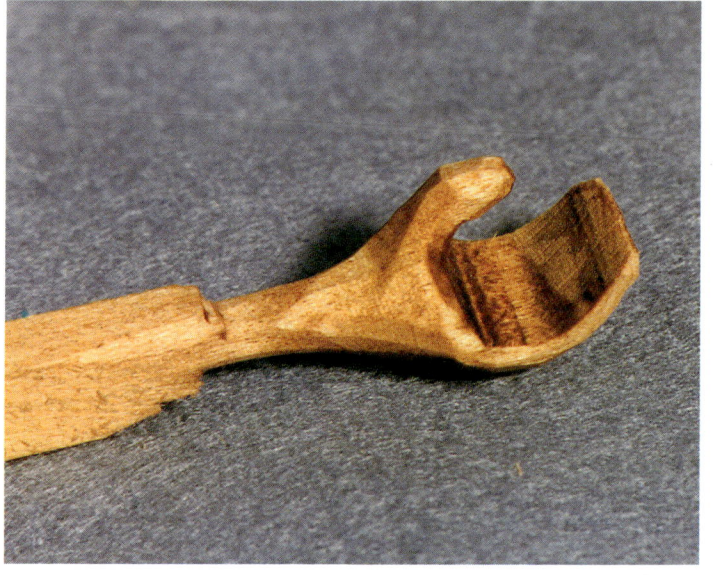

Remove the wood from each hand using a knife or a **#10 6mm "U" gouge**, so the thumbs are well-defined, then round off the sharp edges of the thumbs.

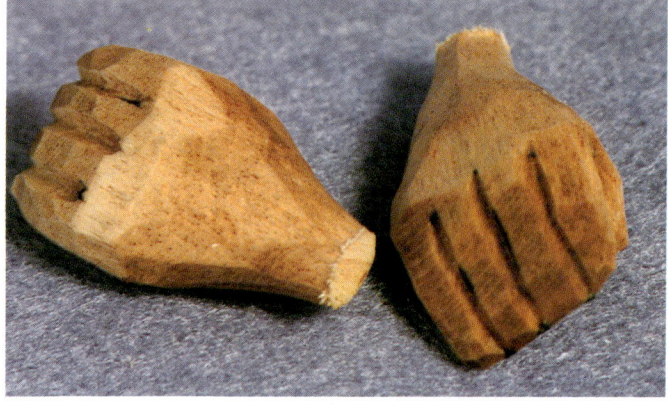

Now, saw or cut the hands apart, so that a section of the connecting wood is still attached to each hand.

51

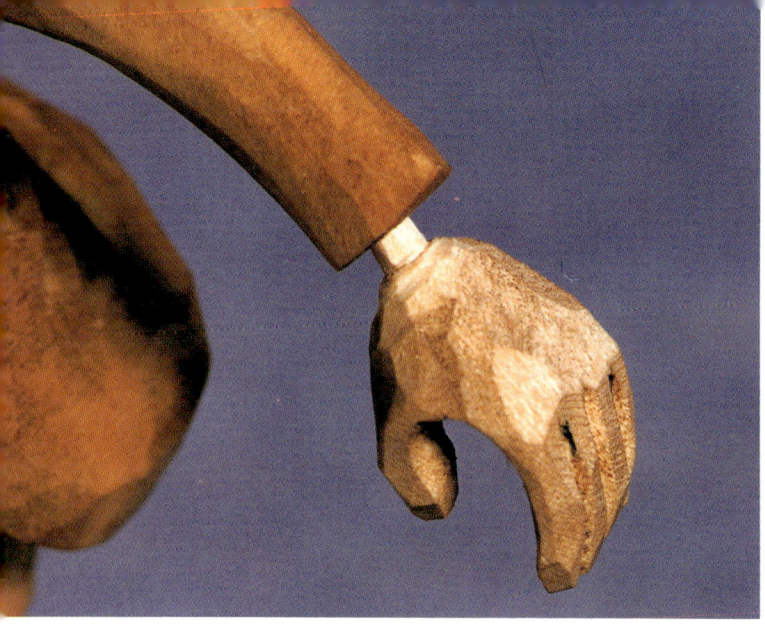

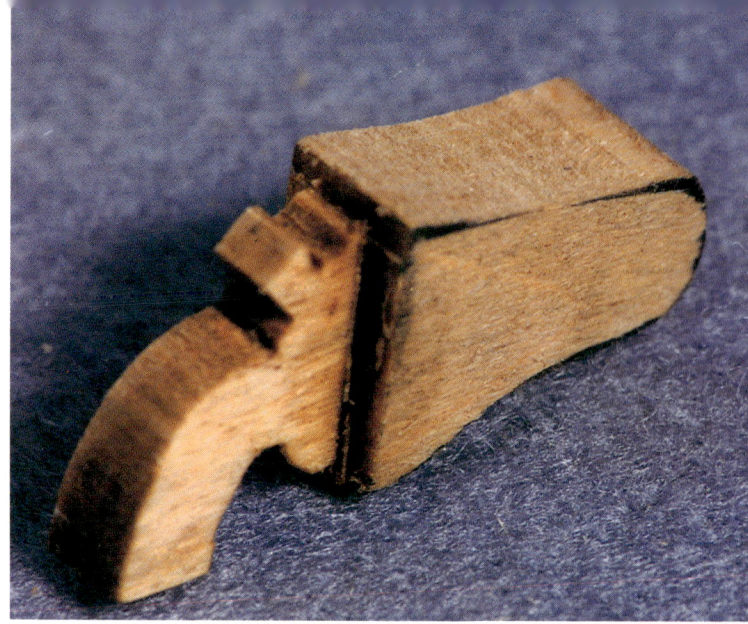

Using your knife, trim the sections of wood down to form a "wrist" that will fit snugly into the holes you drilled earlier in the arms. When done properly, the hand should appear to be coming out of the sleeve. This method allows you to turn the hands in various directions, so your carvings will appear more lifelike. **You may glue the hands in place now, or wait until after they are painted, whichever is easiest for you.**

Draw a line at the top of the holster (both sides), then incise this line about 1/16" deep with your knife. Shave toward the holster from the pistol end, to remove this layer of wood and define the pistol from the holster.

CARVING THE PISTOL

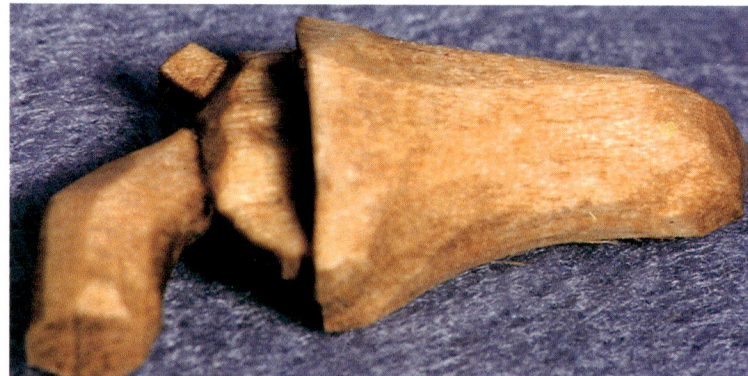

Use your knife to round all the sharp edges on the holster and pistol. (Experienced carvers may add more details to the pistol as they desire).

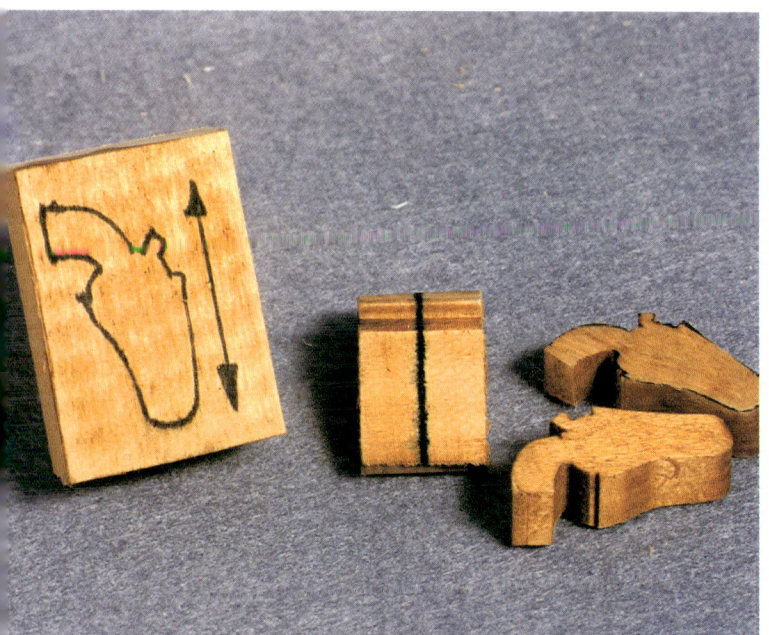

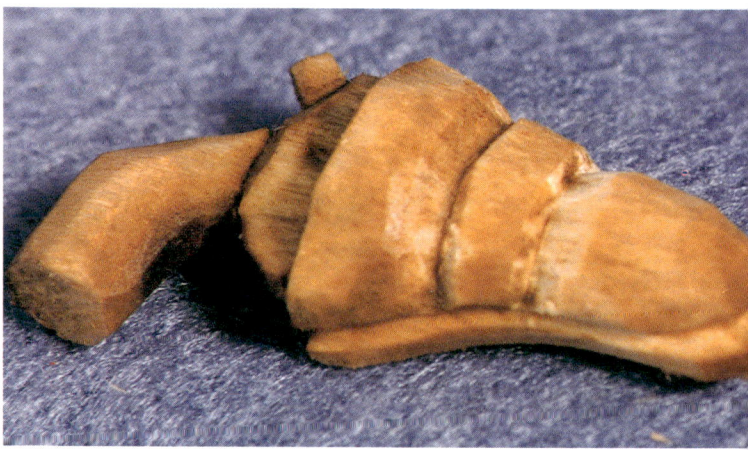

Trace the pistol pattern on a 3/4" thick piece of basswood. Saw it out with a bandsaw or coping saw. Then turn the wood on its side, and saw it in half lengthwise. This will give you two pistols approximately 3/8" thick. One will be used for the project, and the other is your first spare for use on future carvings.

A **#39 1/8" "V" gouge** is used to add a groove around the lower outside edge of the holster, and to make the two grooves across the holster. Using your knife, lightly shave *toward* the two grooves you made across the holster, so this will appear to be a strap, with the holster tucked under it.

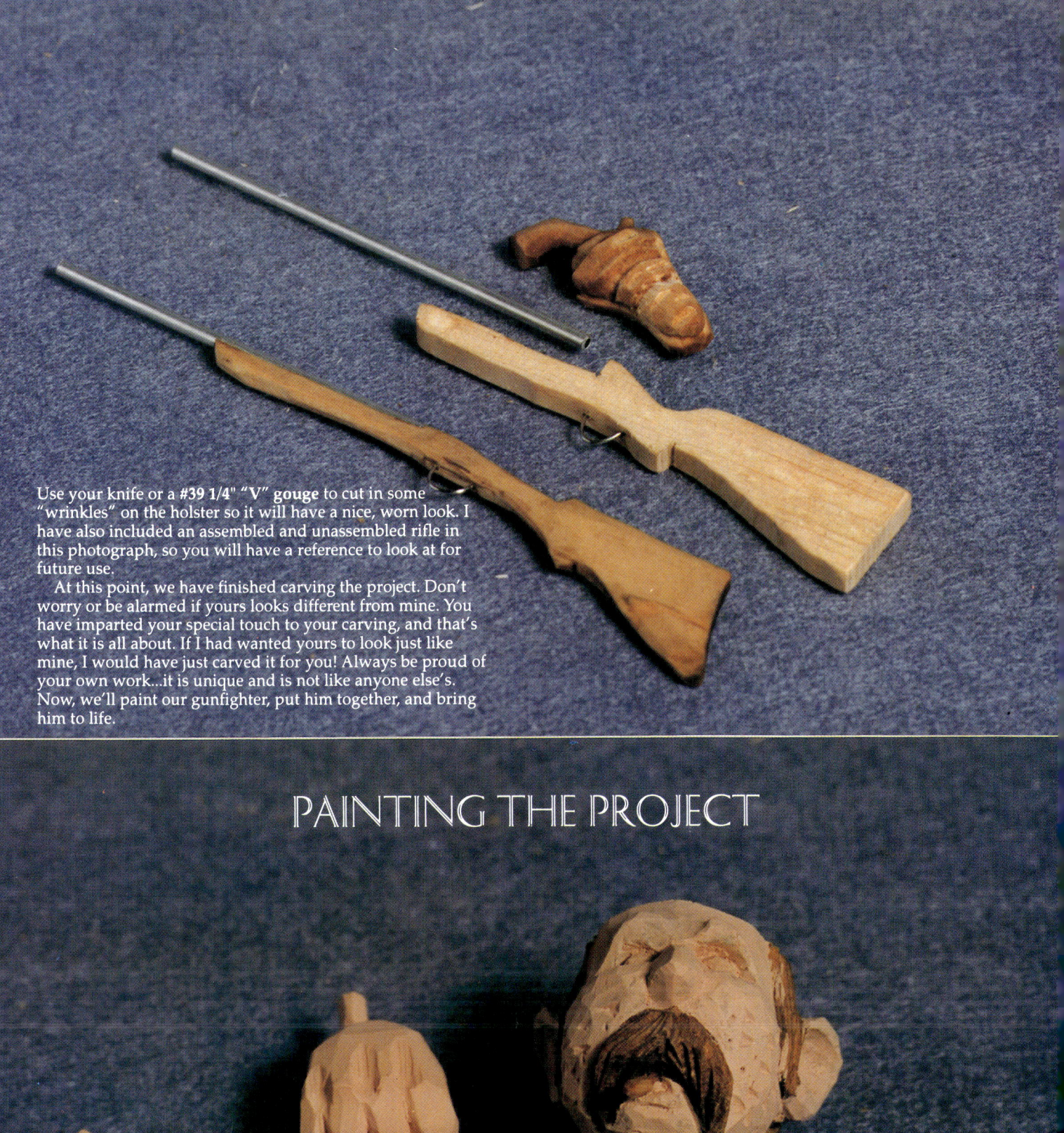

Use your knife or a **#39 1/4" "V" gouge** to cut in some "wrinkles" on the holster so it will have a nice, worn look. I have also included an assembled and unassembled rifle in this photograph, so you will have a reference to look at for future use.

At this point, we have finished carving the project. Don't worry or be alarmed if yours looks different from mine. You have imparted your special touch to your carving, and that's what it is all about. If I had wanted yours to look just like mine, I would have just carved it for you! Always be proud of your own work...it is unique and is not like anyone else's. Now, we'll paint our gunfighter, put him together, and bring him to life.

PAINTING THE PROJECT

Paint the face, ears, neck and hands with FLESHTONE.

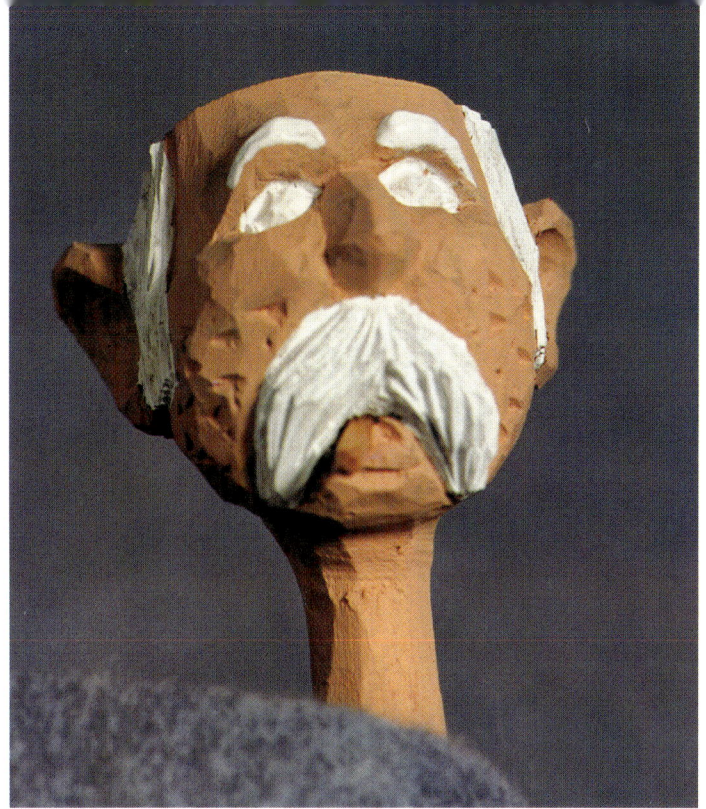

Paint the hair, eyebrows, mustache and eyeballs WHITE. If you used the quilt pin method for eyes, paint them WHITE now.

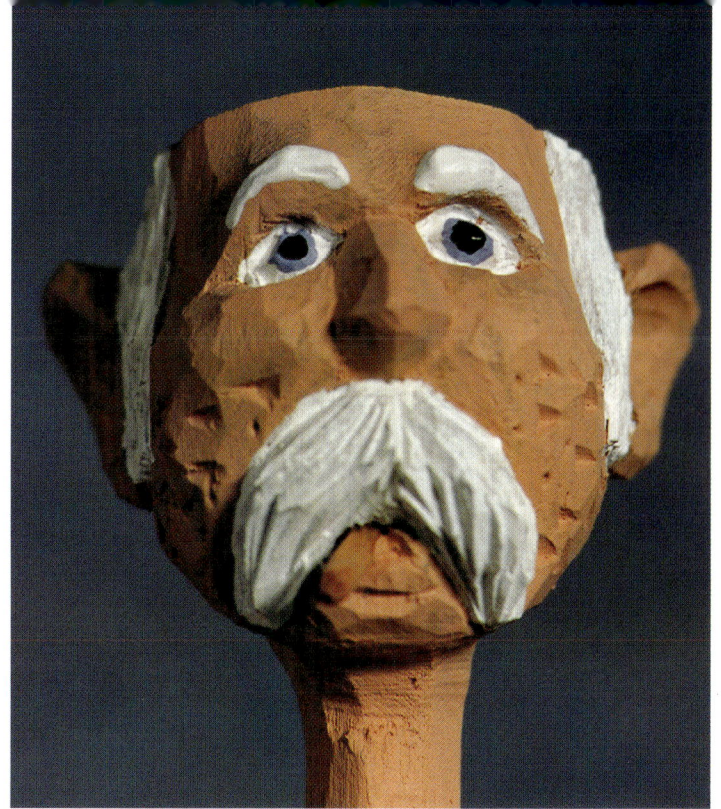

When this is dry, use your fine-tip brush to put a BLACK dot inside the BLUE dot. The placement of the BLUE and BLACK dots will have various effects on the facial expression. Experiment on a piece of scrap wood to discover all the expressions you can create. I personally like to show the eyes rolled upward, looking to one side or the other. You may experiment with different looks and find one that you prefer also.

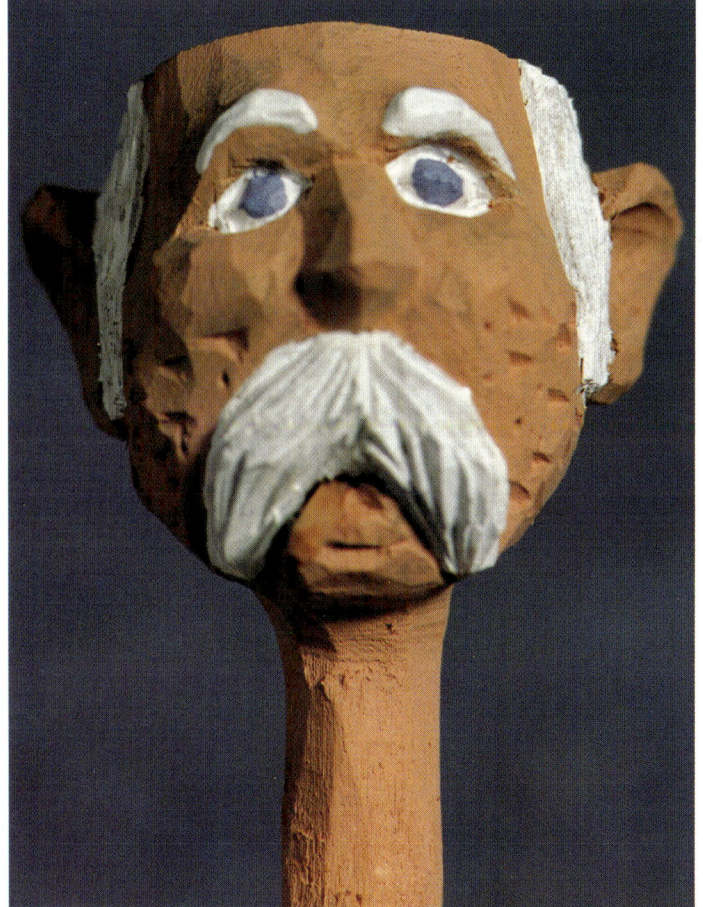

Now take a small, fine-tip brush and put a round dot of BLUE HEAVEN in the center of the eye.

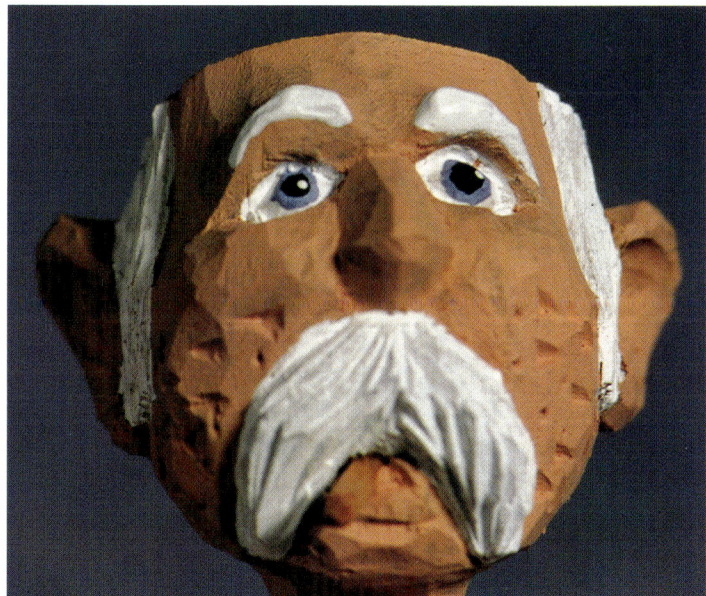

Finally, take a toothpick and put a WHITE highlight on the edge of the BLACK dot. If the eyes are looking to the left, I put the highlight around the 10 o'clock position. If looking to the right, I put the highlight around the 2 o'clock position. When looking straight ahead, as they are here, you can put the highlight at either the 10 o'clock or 2 o'clock position, whichever you prefer. This is another area you can experiment with on a scrap piece of wood, to see the effects of moving the highlight around.

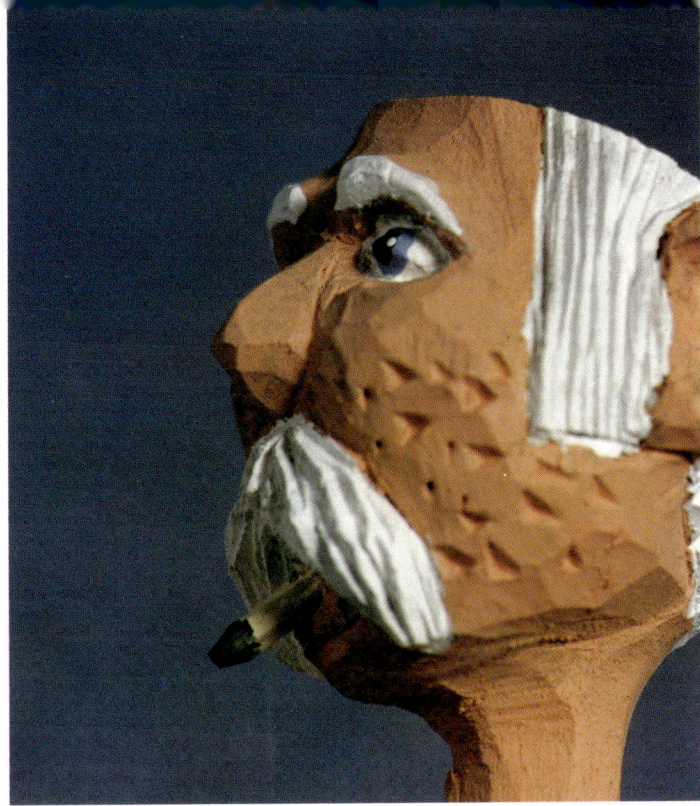

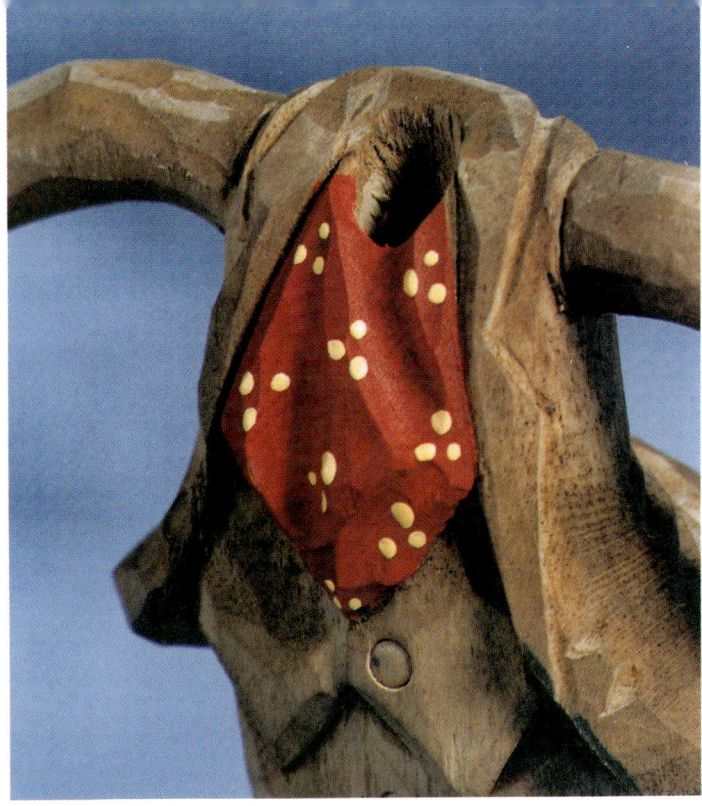

Paint the cigarette ANTIQUE WHITE. Then put a small amount of QUAKER GRAY on the tip to look like ashes.

For the remaining steps of the painting session, remember to **THINK "THIN"**!! Also, remember these are just *suggested* colors. Refer back to the general painting suggestions if you want other ideas and color schemes.

Paint the bandanna CRIMSON with CROCUS YELLOW dots.

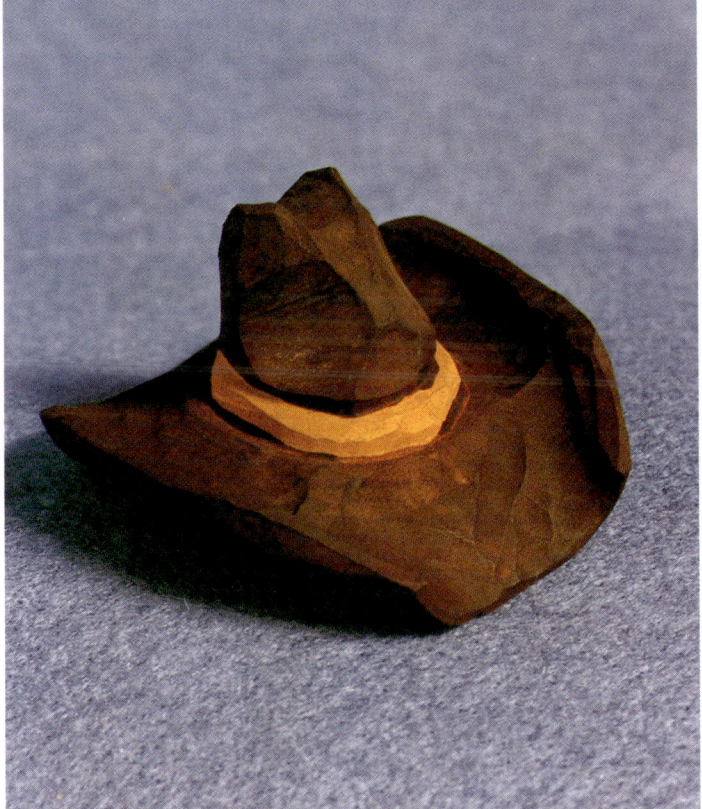

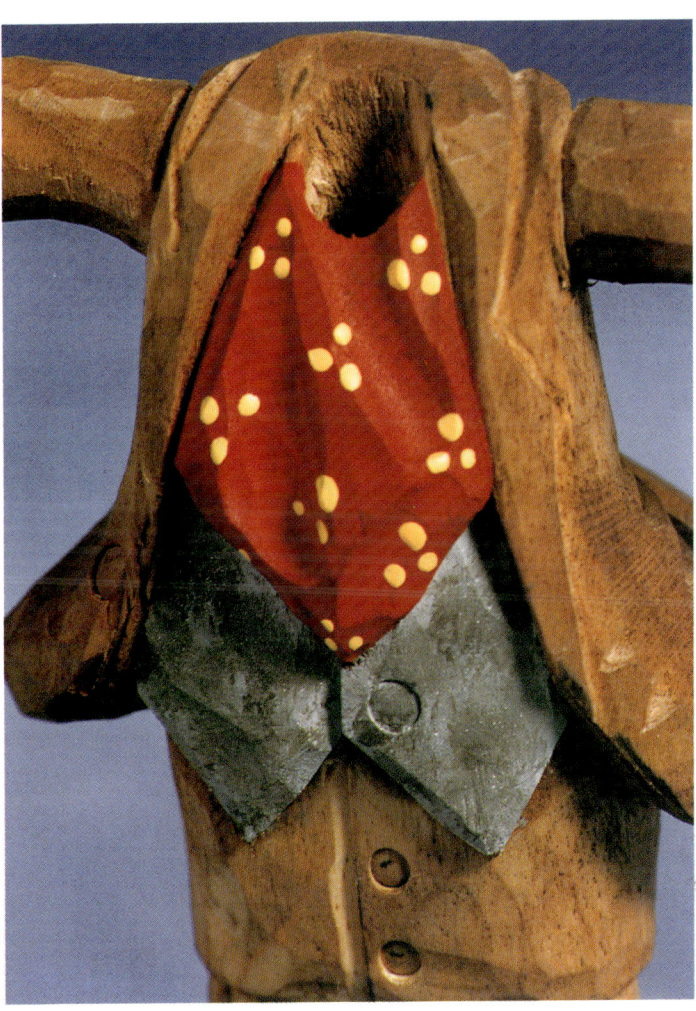

Paint the hatband PIGSKIN, **then** paint the hat BURNT UMBER. (**Do not** paint in the area where the head will be glued in place later).

Paint the vest QUAKER GRAY, with CHARCOAL and SILVER dry-brushed over the QUAKER GRAY to give a brocade effect.

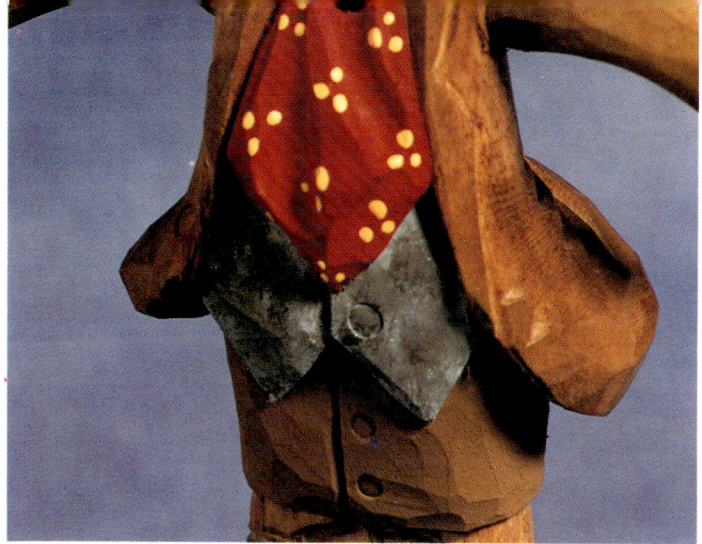

Paint the shirt TERRITORIAL BEIGE.

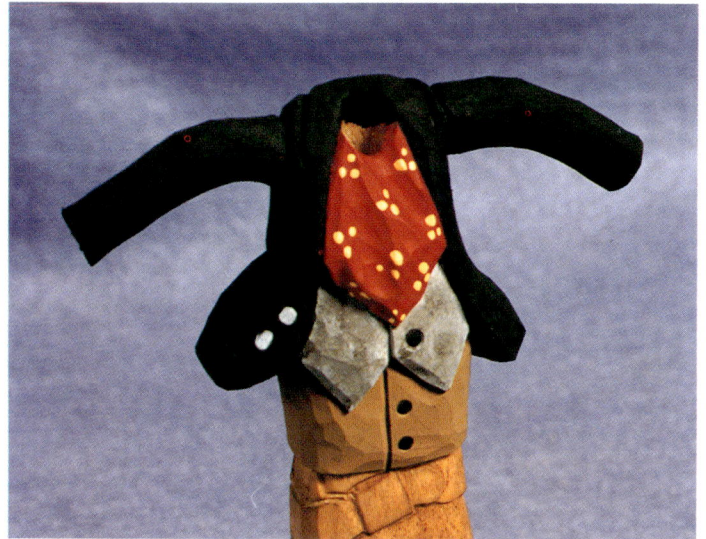

Paint the coat BLACK, then paint the buttons on the vest, shirt, and coat a color of your choice. I used BLACK on the vest and shirt, and SILVER on the coat.

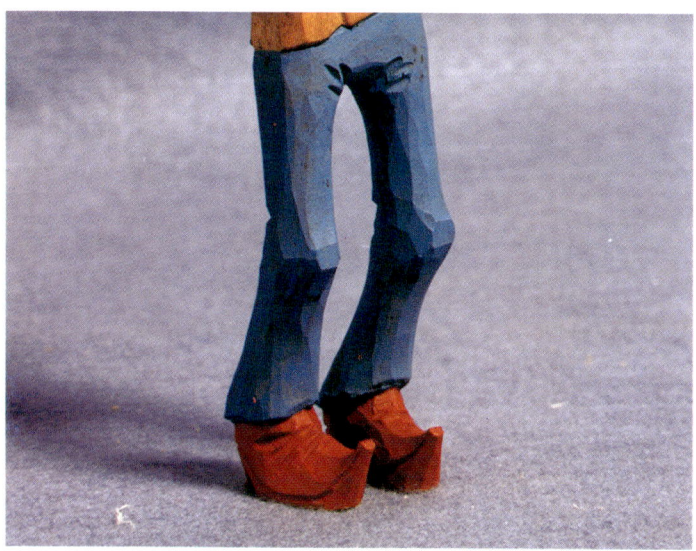

Paint the pants DENIM BLUE, and paint the boots RED OXIDE.

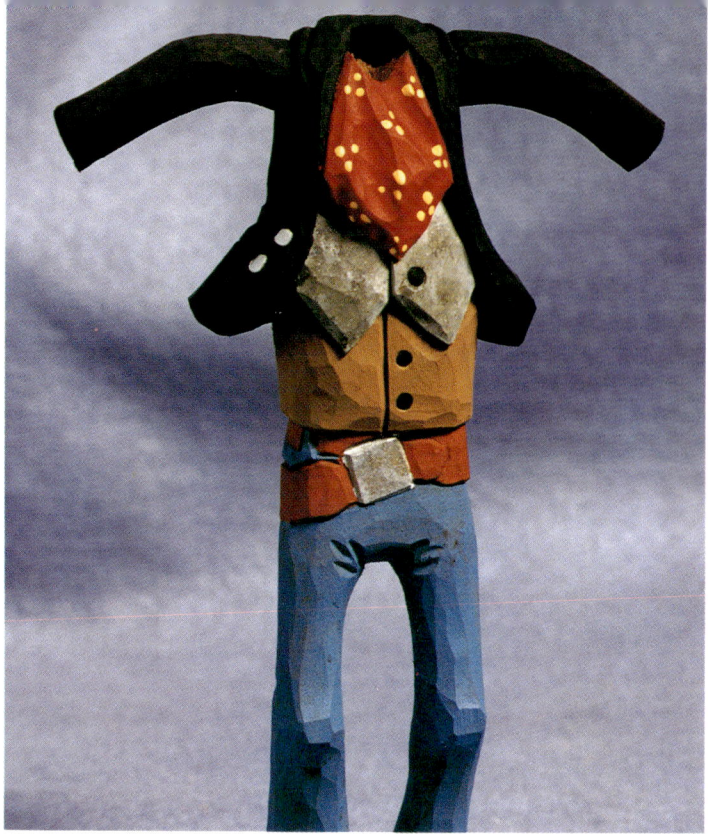

The gunbelt, belt and holster are BURNT SIENNA, and the buckle on the gunbelt is SILVER.

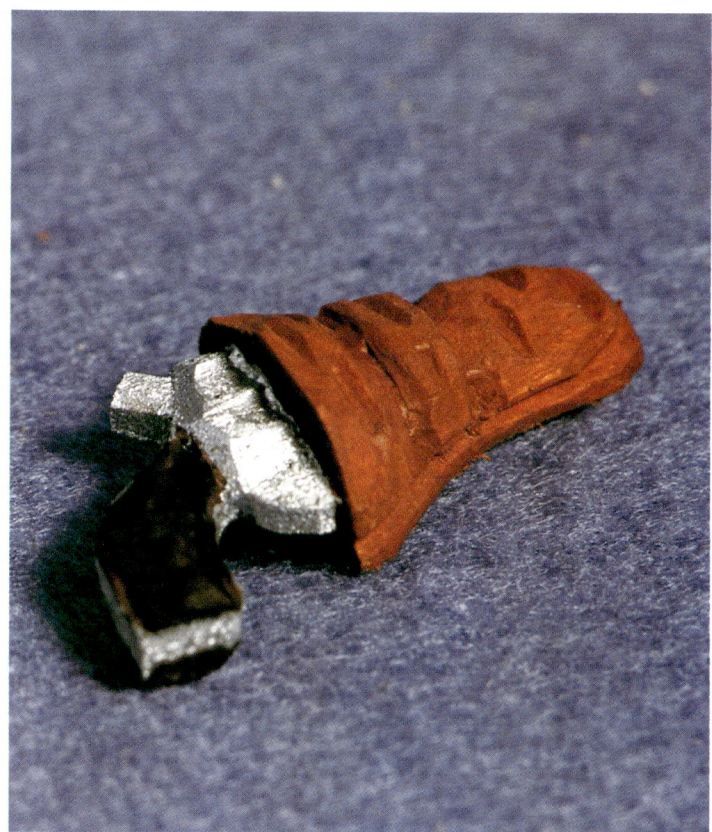

Paint the pistol SILVER with WALNUT hand grips.

We are now through painting the gunfighter. If you wish to antique your project, I have included some instructions below. It is much easier if you do the antiquing **BEFORE** you assemble all the pieces of the carving.

56

ANTIQUING
THE PROJECT

Once the paint is dry, you may want to "age" your gunfighter with an antiquing product in order to help tone down the colors a bit. I have had excellent results using antiquing gels made by Delta Technical Coatings. These are available at hobby and craft stores. They come in various colors, so you can create different effects.

Brush a coat of antiquing gel on the carving, then wipe it off using a damp rag or sponge. It is your option how much you wipe off. After the antiquing is dry, I like to finish my carvings with a coat of brush-on acrylic varnish. Delta Technical Coatings also makes an excellent varnish. I prefer the one that leaves a satin finish. This particular finish is not too flat nor too glossy, but leaves a "soft" look to the completed carving. **(I usually put a coat of varnish on the face, hands and hair area BEFORE I antique the carving).** This will prevent these areas from absorbing too much antiquing color.

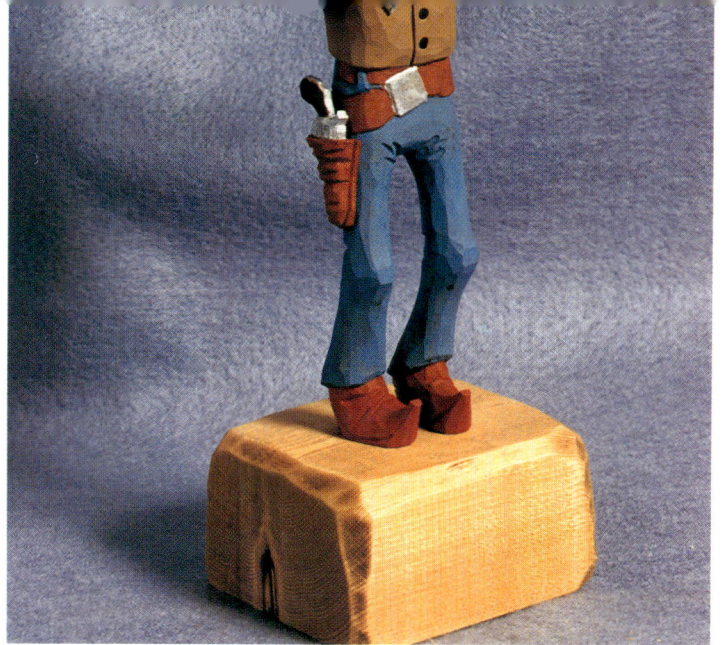

Insert a quilt pin into the side of the right leg, where the gunbelt comes across. Snip it off so about 1/8" protrudes. Put a drop of glue on the pin, and press the pistol in place firmly. The pin will hold the pistol until the glue sets up.

I also made a base for my project from a scrap piece of wood, stained it, and glued the gunfighter to it for more stability.

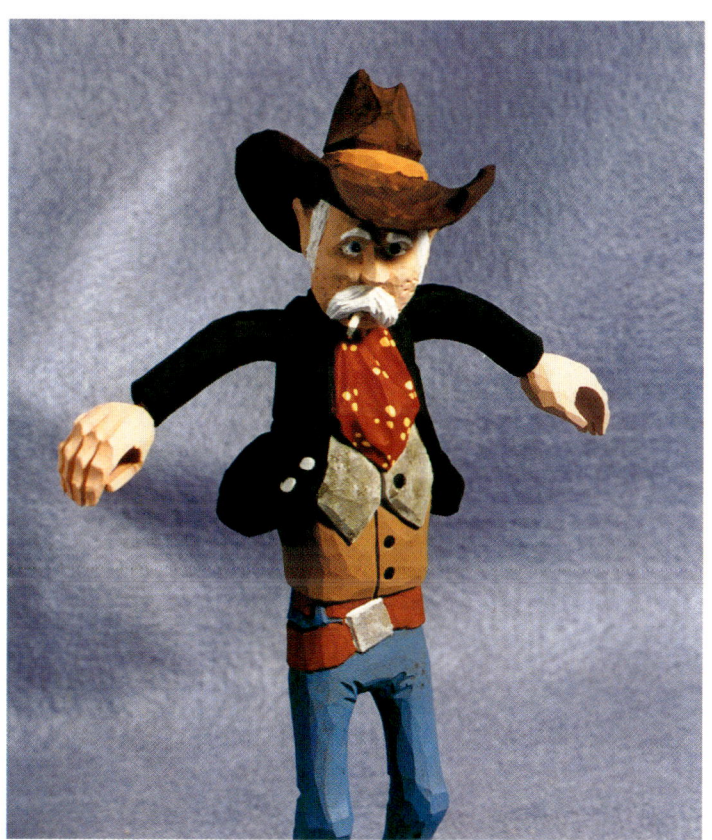

When you are ready to assemble your project, put a drop of glue on the top of the head, and glue the head to the hat. When this is dry, put a drop of glue in the neck hole of the body. Insert the head, and position it looking straight ahead, or looking to the side (your option). I believe the carvings have more "life" to them, when the head is looking to the side. Also, glue the hands in place now, if you didn't do it previously.

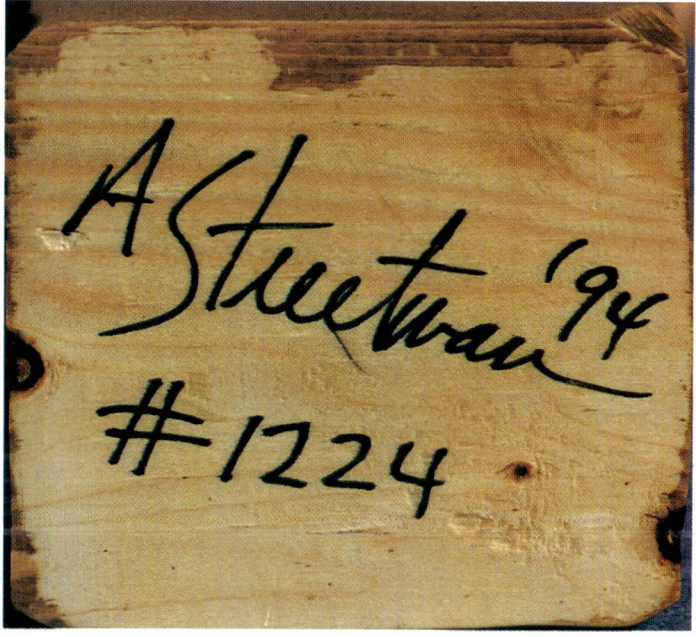

When everything is dry, sign your name, and put the date on the bottom of the carving. After you become a famous carver, your signature will make your carvings more valuable. I also number my carvings, and include this number along with my signature and date. I keep a record book of sequential numbers, along with a brief description of the carving. Many times, collectors will not buy a carving unless it has a signature and a number. As your carvings become more and more "collectible", the lower numbered ones will increase in value to collectors. Your carvings are a reflection of your talent and skill...be proud of that, and put that signature on there so the whole world will know who made that masterpiece! Take a few minutes now to sit back and admire your creation.

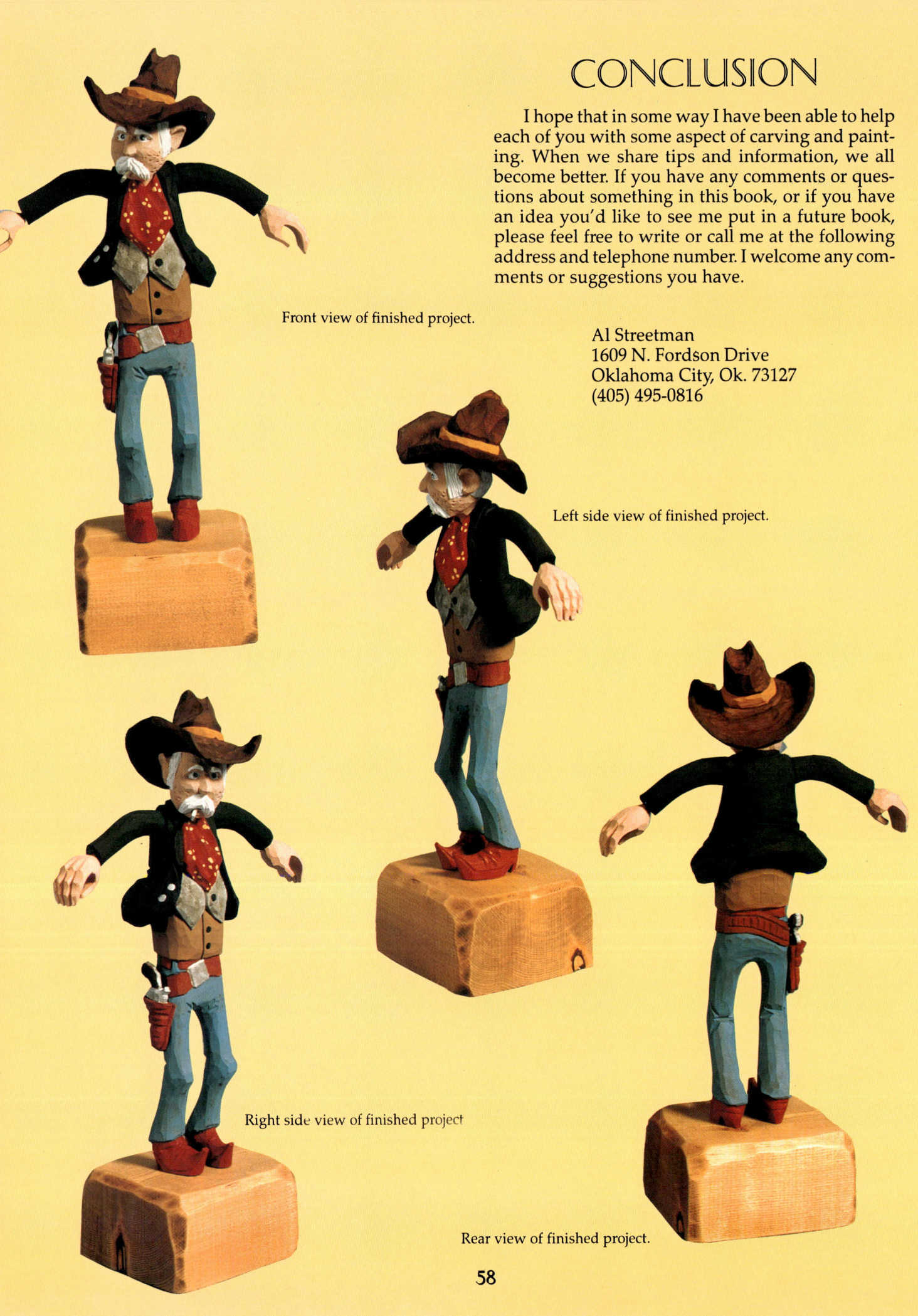

CONCLUSION

I hope that in some way I have been able to help each of you with some aspect of carving and painting. When we share tips and information, we all become better. If you have any comments or questions about something in this book, or if you have an idea you'd like to see me put in a future book, please feel free to write or call me at the following address and telephone number. I welcome any comments or suggestions you have.

Al Streetman
1609 N. Fordson Drive
Oklahoma City, Ok. 73127
(405) 495-0816

Front view of finished project.

Left side view of finished project.

Right side view of finished project

Rear view of finished project.

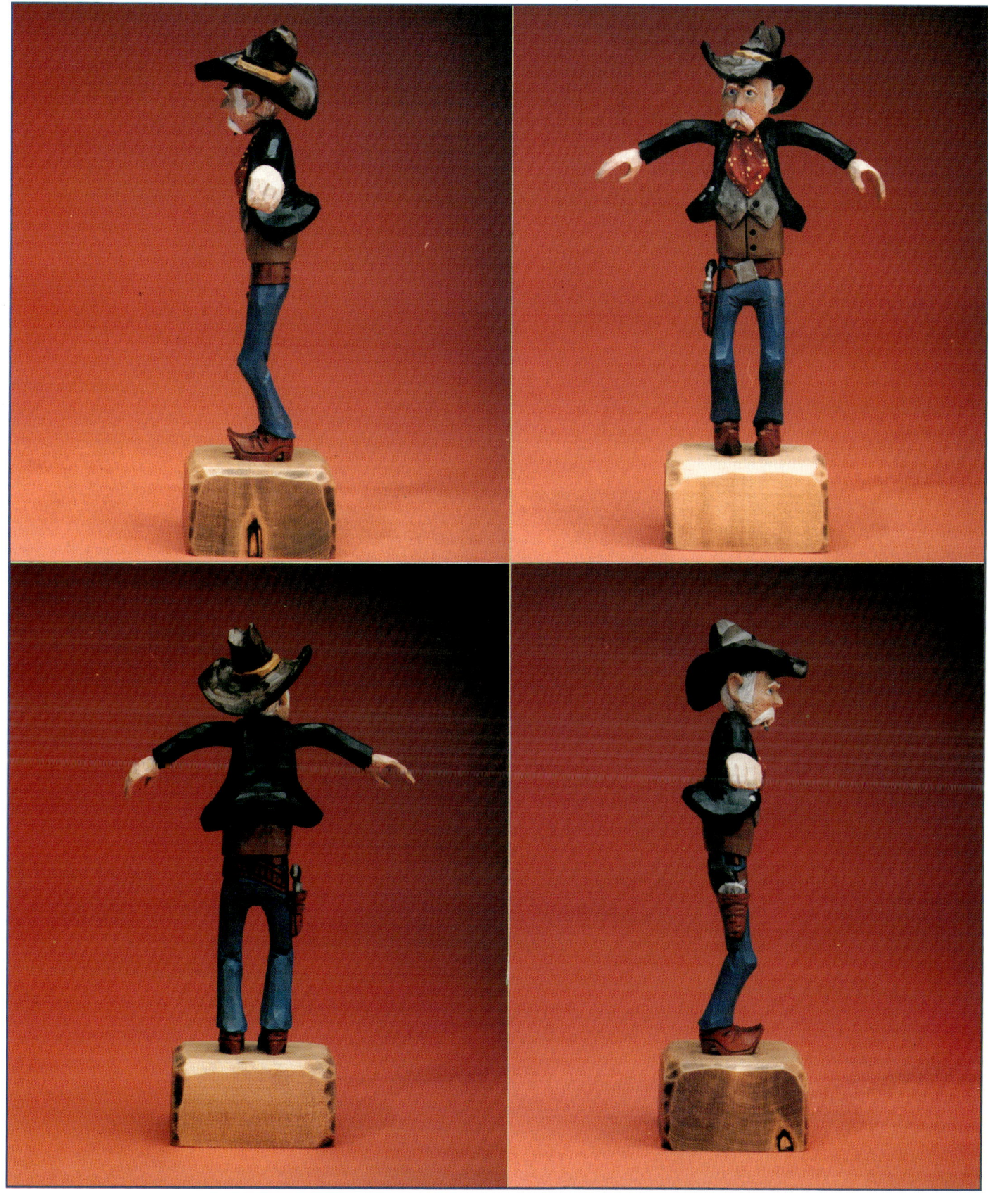

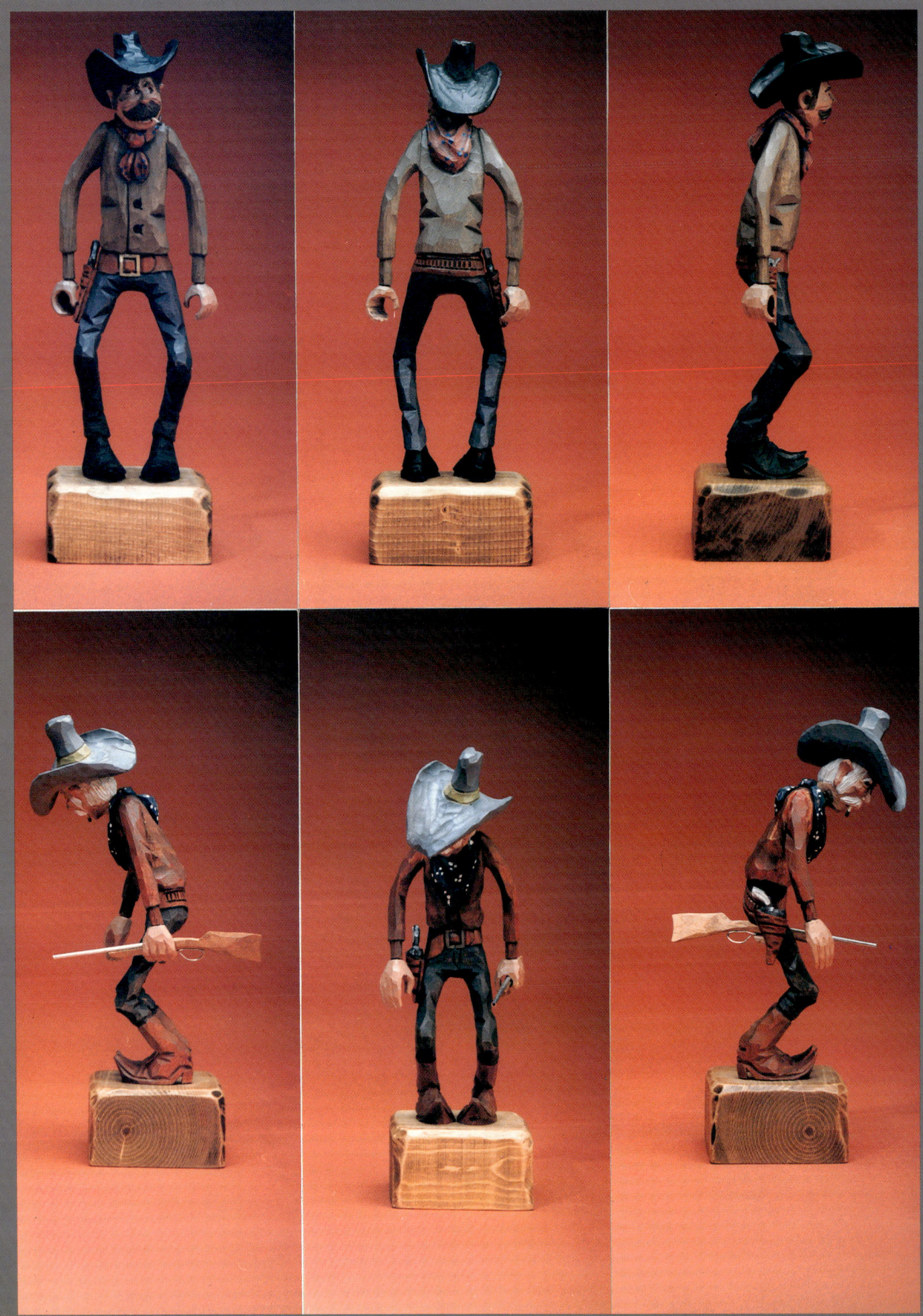

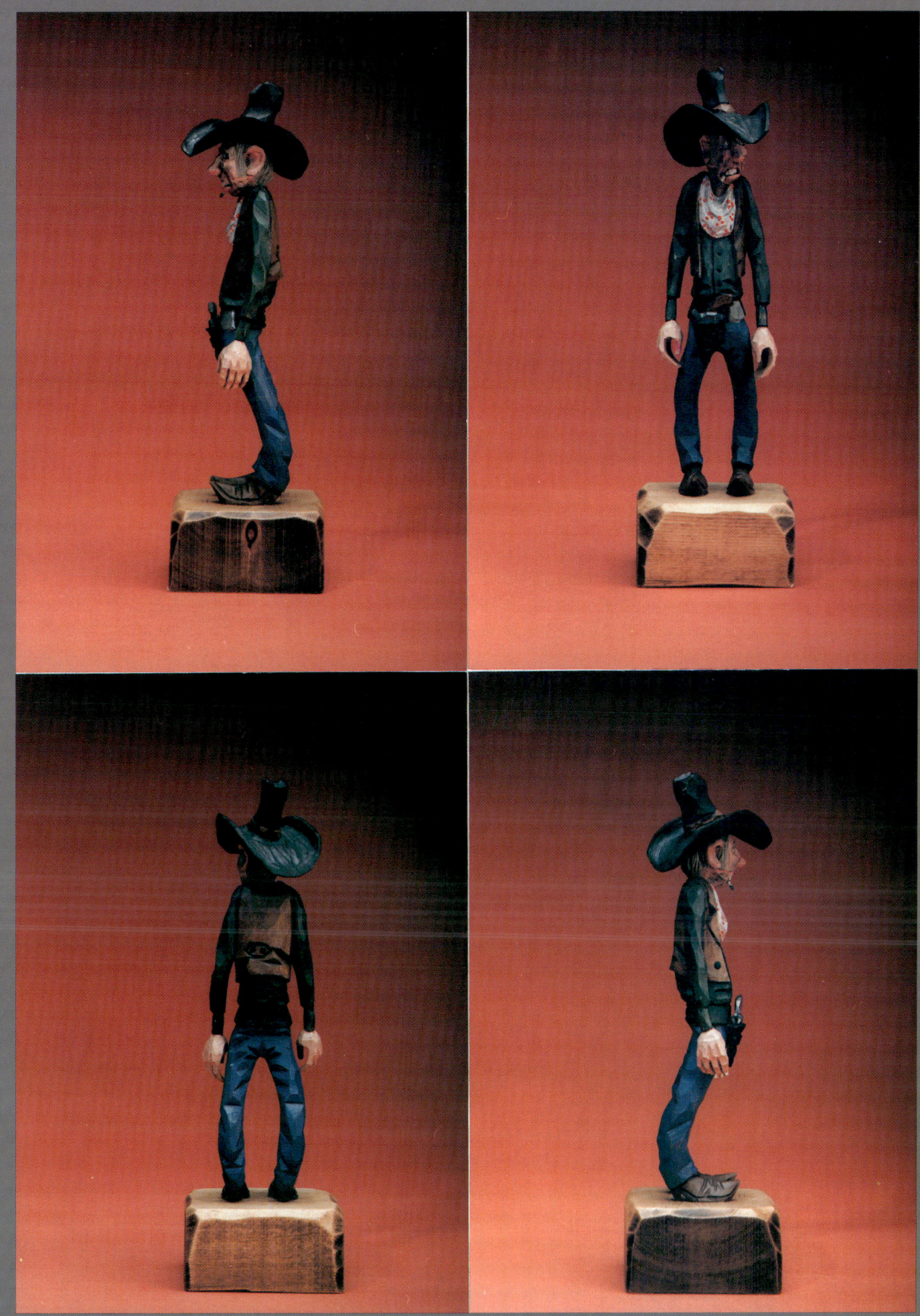

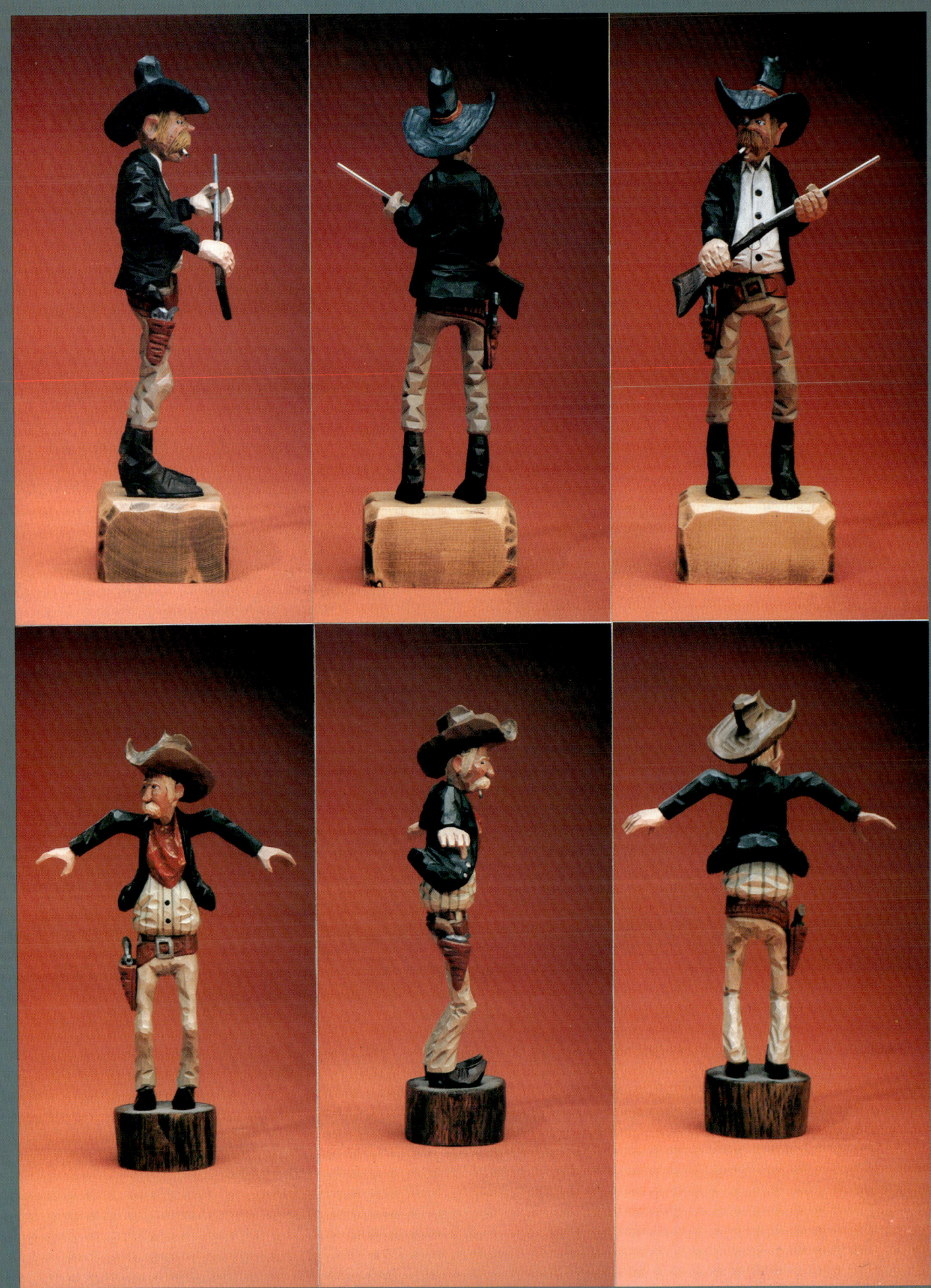

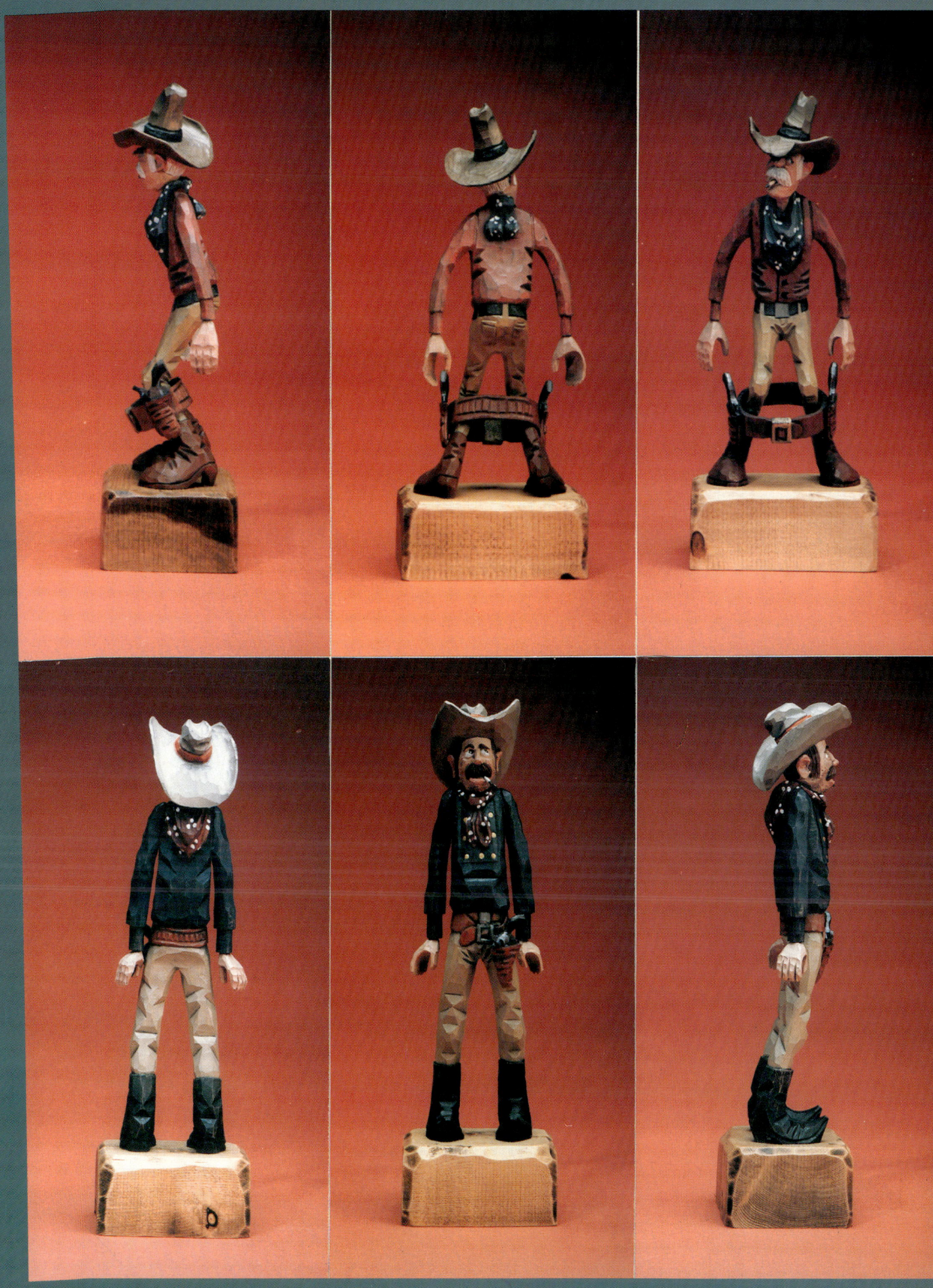

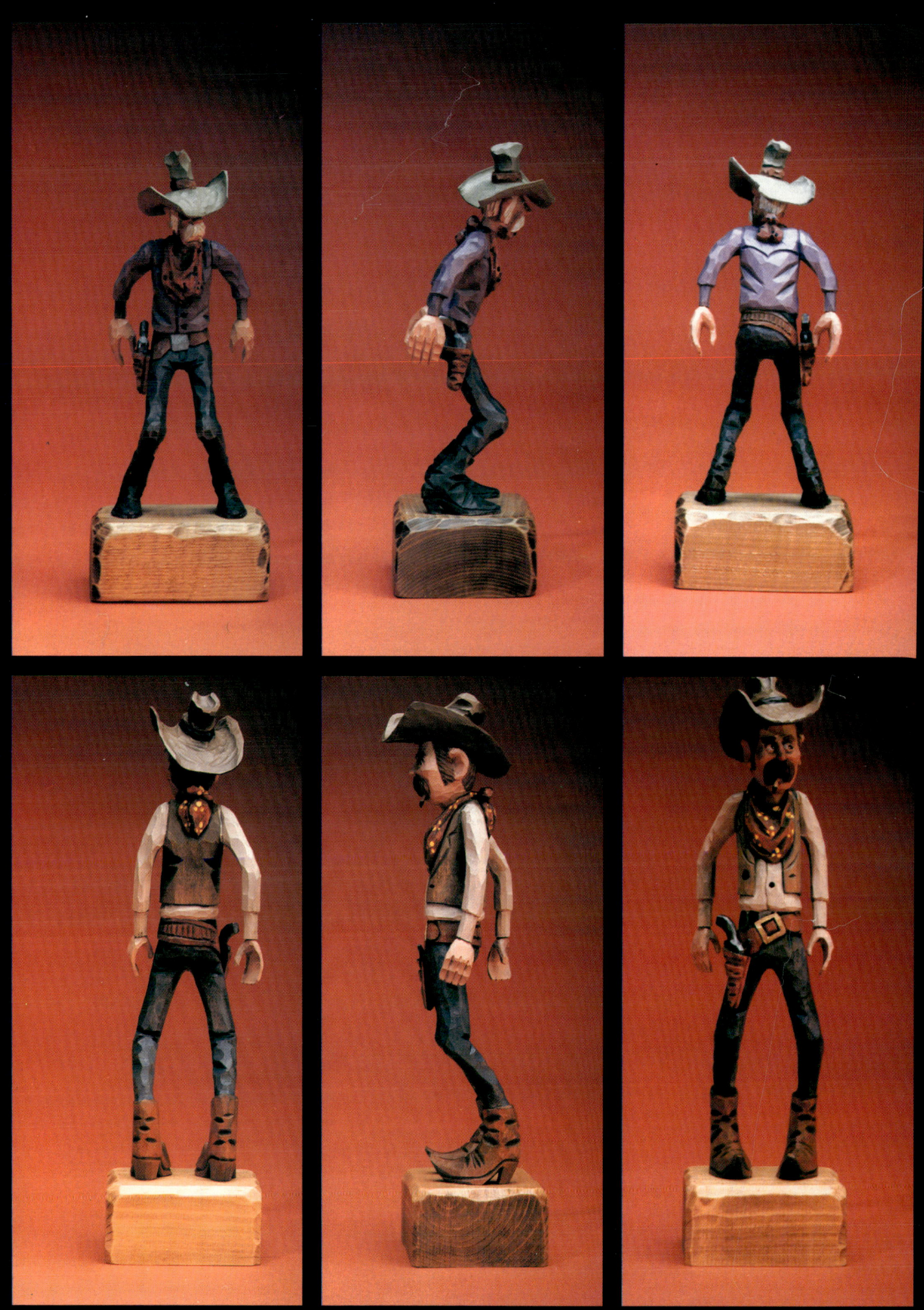